MUHAMMAD: MAN OF GOD

SEYYED HOSSEIN NASR

ABC International Group, Inc.

Book Designer
Liaquat Ali

Library of Congress Cataloging in Publication Data

Nasr, Seyyed Hossein
Muhammad: Man of God. 1st US ed.

Includes bibliographical note and index.
1. Islam. 2. Muhammad, Prophet, d. 632.. I. Nasr, Seyyed Hossein.
II. Title.
BP75.A76 1995
297'.63-dc20

ISBN: 1-56744-501-2

Published by
ABC International Group, Inc.

Distributed by
KAZI Publications, Inc. (USA)
3023 W. Belmont Avenue
Chicago IL 60618
Tel: (773) 267-7001; FAX: (773) 267-7002

Contents

TRANSLITERATION

Arabic Letters

symbol	transliteration
ء	ʼ
ب	b
ت	t
ث	th
ج	j
ح	ḥ
خ	kh
د	d
ذ	dh
ر	r
ز	z
س	s
ش	sh
ص	ṣ
ض	ḍ
ط	ṭ
ظ	ẓ
ع	ʻ
غ	gh
ف	f
ق	q
ك	k
ل	l
م	m
ن	n
ه	h
و	w
ي	y
ة	ah; at (*construct state*)
ال	(*article*) al- *and* 'l (*even before the antepalatals*)

Long Vowels

اى	ā
و	ū
ي	ī

Short Vowels

َ	a
ُ	u
ِ	i

Diphthongs

ـَو	au
ـَي	ai
ـِيّ	iy (Final Form ī)
ـُوّ	uww (Final Form ū)

Persian Letters

پ	p
چ	ch
ژ	zh
گ	g

Yā Ḥabīb-Allāh (O Beloved of God)

O Seal of Prophecy, Pillar of Existence,
O Prophet of God, His beloved,
At once praised and praising His Majesty,
Unlettered, yet fount of all knowledge.
O most perfect of His creatures, drawn near,
In that Nocturnal Ascent which crowned thy earthly life,
The being for whom He created the heavens,
The servant of the One, yet master of the world,
Whose light sustains that spectrum of forms,
Which constitutes the abode of our existence.
In humility I bow before thy grandeur,
Asking thy forgiveness in seeking to describe,
In words so unworthy of the dust of thy feet,
An inkling of the blinding light of thy life,
Which illuminated the land of Hijaz and beyond,
Creating an aura that continues to light,
The path of those for whom thou art the guide.
Thy green flag shall continue to wave,
Unto the darkest hours of historic time,
Until the Truth of which thou wert and remain
The supreme messenger and defender,
Manifests its full glory once again,
Amidst the human misery of a world gone astray.
O Muhammad whose praise is sung by the Lord,
As by His angels and, too, servants on earth,
I need thy successor to achieve this arduous task,
Of describing, however humbly, the contours of a life,
Which remain forever the perfect model,
Revealing in all its nobility and beauty,
What it means to be truly human.

بسم الله الرحمن الرحيم
١٤١٣

PREFACE

In the Name of God, the Merciful, the Compassionate. This short study of the life of the Blessed Prophet of Islam is neither a new historical analysis nor yet another purely devotional sketch of the earthly career of God's last prophet. There are already numerous historical studies of him in European languages, written not only by Western scholars, but also by Muslims either writing in these languages or having their work translated into these tongues, especially English. There are more specialized studies devoted to him as statesman, military commander, political leader, etc. Moreover, some biographies, which may be called devotional literature, are available in English although works which bring out the spiritual significance of the Blessed Prophet and the inner meaning of the various episodes of his life are rare. Despite existing works therefore, there still exists the need for biographies which would take into consideration the spiritual dimensions as well as the more factual and historical elements of the life of the person who changed human history.

The present study aims to be a humble step in this direction and seeks to fulfill the need for a short biography which would take into consideration the known historical facts and their spiritual significance while preserving the traditional Islamic point of view and explaining certain elements of this exemplary life which have been cast into doubt by the modernized, skeptical mind. This monograph is addressed primarily to the young Muslim reader who has no access to the traditional sources and is yet in need of a traditional and at the same time contemporary presentation of the life of the Blessed Prophet.

The pen of the author of these lines is incapable of depicting the grandeur of the subject it has treated. It is only hoped that this humble effort will give at least an inkling of the greatness, majesty and nobility of life of the being whom God has called a mercy unto the world. Whatever has been accomplished is due to His help while the faults are our own. We ask forgiveness for the shortcomings of this treatment and realize only too well how difficult indeed is the task of depicting in contemporary language something of the grandeur of a being the dimensions of whose personality exceed the ken of imagination of the majority of those who live in the modern world and who have become accustomed to the mediocrity characterizing this world.

We wish to point out the laudable efforts of the late Commander Husayn, the director of the of the Muhammadi Trust which first published this work and which has already done much to make possible a better understanding of Islam in the West and to make available in the English language authentic works on Islam as well as KAZI Publications, Inc. for printing the revised edition of this work.

wa' Llāhu a'lam

INTRODUCTION

Lo! God and His Angels shower blessings on the Prophet. O ye who believe! Ask blessings on him and salute him with a worthy salutation (Quran—XXXIII: 56—Pickthall translation.)

[The Blessed Prophet] is the chief of created beings, the most noble of creatures, the mercy of the universe, the purest of mankind, and completion of the revolution of the ages, Muhammad Mustafa (upon whom be blessings and peace!) the intercessor, the obeyed, the gracious Prophet, the bountiful, the majestic, the affable, the sealed. How can the rampart of the faith totter which has thee for a prop? What can he fear from the waves of the sea who has Noah for his pilot? He reached the pinnacle of glory through his perfections; he illuminated the darkness of chaos by his splendor; all his habits were elegant; blessings be upon him and on his followers. (Gulistān of Sa'dī—based on the translations of F. Gladwin and J. Ross.)

The seal of prophets, the most perfect of all of God's creatures and the beloved (*ḥabīb*) of God, Muhammad—may peace and blessings be upon him and his family—was born in Makkah on the 17th, or according to some the

12th, of Rabīʿ al-Awwal of the Year of the Elephant in 570 A.D. (when the Abyssinian army invading Arabia was defeated). This adornment of the created order was also named Aḥmad, Muṣṭāfā, ʿAbdallāh, Abu'l-Qāsim, and also given the title al-Amīn, the trusted one. Each of his names and titles speaks of an aspect of his blessed being. He was, as the etymological meaning of Muḥammad and Aḥmad reveals, the glorified or praised one; he was Muṣṭāfā, the chosen one, ʿAbdallāh, the perfect servant of God, and later as the father of Qāsim, Abu'l-Qāsim. He was to become not only the prophet (*nabī*) and messenger (*rasūl*) of God, but also the friend of God and a mercy sent unto the world for as the Noble Quran states, "*We sent thee not save as a mercy for the peoples*" (Quran—XXI:107).

2 EARLY LIFE

The Prophet of God was born in a city whose sanctuary, the Ka'bah, was built by the prophet Abraham, the patriarch of monotheism and the father of both the Arabs and the Jews. But this ancient religious center had remained on the side of the main theater of human civilizations and the battleground between major world powers. The main events of history in the region, the conquest of Babylon by Cyrus and the founding of the Persian Empire, the conquests of Alexander, the foundation of the Roman Empire, the birth and ascent to heaven of Christ, the termination of ancient Egyptian civilization, the destruction of the Temple of Jerusalem, the founding of the Byzantine Empire and its constant battles with the Persians to the East had also by-passed Makkah. Meanwhile, over the millennia, the original monotheistic message of Abraham had become forgotten in Arabia and the vast majority of Arabs had fallen into a state of idolatry of the worst kind. They had forgotten the Truth and fallen into the age of ignorance (*al-jāhiliyyah*) which formed the immediate background for the rise of Islam. The only exception, besides the small number of Christians and Jews residing in Arabia, were the few solitary souls who had remembered Abraham's primordial religion, people whom the Noble Quran calls the *ḥanīfs* (or *ḥunafā'*).

Parallel with this religious decadence, the Makkah of this period, preceding the descent of the Islamic revelation, was experiencing great economic prosperity and wealth which only increased the constant rivalry between various tribes and, in fact, augmented the power of the tribe ruling over Makkah which even then was the site of pilgrimage for tribes from all over Arabia as well as being the economic center of the land. As the hands of destiny would have it, the tribe into which the Blessed Prophet was born was none other than the tribe which dominated the city of Makkah and the center of pilgrimage and, therefore, wielded special power throughout Arabia.

The Blessed Prophet was born in the highly aristocratic and influential family of the Banū Kinānah whose subdivision, the Quraysh, constituted his immediate tribe. His own family was a branch of the Quraysh called the Banū Hāshim named after Hāshim the patriarch of the family who was a very prominent person in Makkah and traded widely, even as far away as Syria and Yemen. His son, 'Abd al-Muṭṭalib, the grandfather of the Prophet of Islam, apportioned the water of the Zamzam and was the custodian of the Ka'bah, the house of God, which despite being blemished by idols made by human hand, was still the sanctuary of Abraham and, in fact, Adam, as well, the first prophet and father of mankind. 'Abd al-Muṭṭalib had once had a visionary dream which foretold of the birth of the being who was to bring the word of God, the Noble Quran, to mankind. 'Abd al-Muṭṭalib saw in this vision a tree growing out of his back, a tree whose upper branches reached the skies and whose side branches stretched from the East to the West. A light brighter than the sun shone from this tree and both the Arabs and the Persians worshipped it. The interpreters of dreams told him that a person would be born in his family who would illumine the East and West and who would be the prophet of both the Arabs and the Persians. The son of ʻAbd al-Muṭṭalib, named ʻAbdallāh, married Amīnah bint Wahb and although he died soon, his wife gave birth to Muḥammad—upon whom be blessings and peace—a short while thereafter. Amīnah did not experience any of the usual signs of bearing a child and had visions and auditory experiences of an exceptional nature at the moment of the birth of the being about whom God has said, "O Adam, had here not been Muḥammad, I would have created neither you nor the earth and the sky" (*Ḥadīth qudsī*).

This purest and most noble of human beings exhibited exceptional qualities while a small child. He was gentle and mild and loved peace and solitude even at a tender age. It is said that when he was four years old, two angels opened his breast and washed it with snow, which means that his inner being was already purified at a young age by God's angelic forces. He was then put on a scale and weighed against ordinary people. No matter how many people were put on the other side of the scale, he still weighed more, which means that it was he who counted most before the eyes of God and who one day was to guide his people towards God. In the eyes of the Divinity, humanity is seen and judged as members of the religious communities founded by prophets sent by God, religious communities which Islam calls *ummah*. In His eyes the worth of the community is determined by the degree that it follows its prophet and the message sent for the community through him. That is why in the eyes of God the prophet "weighs more," symbolically speaking, than all of his followers put together.

The future Prophet was given to Ḥalīmah, his foster mother, of the tribe of Banū Sa'd and lived in the countryside with the tribe for some time. At the age of six he lost his mother and he also came back to Makkah where, as a complete orphan, he was brought up first by 'Abd al-Muṭṭalib and two years later when he died, by the Blessed Prophet's uncle, Abū Ṭalib, who loved him dearly. In this household, which was also the household of 'Alī, Abū Ṭalib's son, the Blessed Prophet passed his most sensitive age of adolescence and early manhood. At the age of nine, he was already a contemplative person, spending much time alone, meditating in the desert upon the beauty of nature and the wonders of creation. He thought often of the meaning of human life and was aware of the noble nature which the human being carries within himself if only he were to become aware of this inner and primordial nature. It is said that at this tender age when one day his playmates asked him to come and play with them, he responded, "Man is created for a more noble purpose than indulgence in frivolous activities."

At the age of twelve, the Blessed Prophet was taken by his uncle to Syria and Basra along with the trade caravan which usually followed the route between Makkah and these cities. Traditional Islamic sources speak of the Christian monk Buḥayrah who met the Blessed Prophet during this journey. Buḥayrah was a Christian ascetic who was said to have possessed inner or esoteric knowledge. Usually he disregarded caravans which passed by his monastery, but this time he invited the whole caravan in and when the leaders alone came in, he asked especially for the young man who was traveling with the caravan to join them. When he saw the Blessed Prophet, he uncovered his shoulder and pointed to a mark in the middle which, according to traditional teachings, was the mark of prophecy. He predicted that the young boy would grow to be a great prophet and to illuminate the world.

In the decade between 580 and 590, when he reached the age of twenty, the Blessed Prophet accompanied his uncle in many different activities including not only trade, but also wars which took place intermittently between the Quraysh and the Banū Ḥawāzin. This period provided him with many opportunities to learn about trade and economic dealings as well as different aspects of human nature which he was to observe in the conditions of war and peace, in moments of tranquility as well as tension or danger. During this whole period, he exhibited a purity of character, a sense of honesty and such trustworthiness that the people around him came to call him the Trusted One or al-Amīn. He became widely known in the Makkan community for these qualities.

3 The Prophet's Marriage

It was this outstanding reputation of uprightness, honesty, objectivity and sense of justice that led a wealthy and noble woman merchant of Makkah, Khadījah, who was a widow, to invite Muḥammad—upon whom be blessings and peace—to take charge of her affairs. At the instigation and advice of his uncle, the Blessed Prophet accepted this offer and at the age of twenty-five took charge of her caravans which traveled between Makkah and Syria and Basra. His countenance, character, manners and dealings were so impressive to Khadījah that she proposed marriage to him, a proposal which he accepted since she was a person of great nobility of character and beauty of soul. When they married he was twenty-five and she forty. The orphan who had suffered so much loneliness, financial difficulty and hardship in everyday life was blessed by God with a wife who loved him dearly, who believed completely in him and who had the means of providing the kind of social status in Makkah which would later allow him to carry out his religious activities on a wider basis and, after the call of heaven came to him, to establish firmly the seeds of the religious community of Islam.

The marriage with Khadījah was of very great significance in the life of the Prophet of Islam for it provided for him the companion upon whom he could rely completely in the most difficult period of his life and who was endowed with the necessary moral and spiritual virtues to act as the perfect wife of God's most perfect creature and the mother of the prophetic family—the *Ahl al-bayt*—whose light was later to illuminate the world.

Khadījah had been married twice before marrying the Blessed Prophet and had had two sons and one daughter from her earlier marriages. She was also to bear several children for the Blessed Prophet. Her first son from him was named Qāsim (hence the title of Abu'l-Qāsim given to the Prophet of Islam), but he died when two years old. The second son named 'Abdallāh and surnamed al-Ṭāhir and al-Ṭayyib also died in infancy. The Blessed Prophet had four daughters: Zaynab, Ruqayyah, Umm Kulthūm and Fāṭimah, all of whom in contrast to the sons lived to the age of maturity. The youngest daughter, Fāṭimah, was of special sanctity, a soul made for paradise, who only suffered in this world below. She became the wife of 'Alī and is the mother of the Shi'ite Imams and the *sharīfs* or descendants of the Prophet throughout the world. She, of course, played a special role in the religious galaxy surrounding the spiritual Sun which was the Prophet of Islam. Her role in Islamic piety and religious practice stands in a unique position among all the children of the Blessed Prophet and Khadījah and in fact all Muslim women. She symbolizes the spiritual fruit of that perfect marriage which was that of the Blessed Prophet and Khadījah, a marriage which was so complete and in a sense absolute that the Blessed Prophet did not marry another wife as long as Khadījah was alive. This fact is particularly important since she was fifteen years older than he and polygamy was a very common practice in Arabia, as in most other parts of the world, at that time.

A word should in fact be said about the marriages of the Blessed Prophet and his attitude toward sexuality, which is, of course, the basis of the Islamic attitude in this domain, since so much criticism has been made of it by Western writers. Sexuality has two aspects. It can be a dangerous passion which harms both body and soul or it can be a positive gift from God necessary not only for procreation but also as a means of drawing closer to Him. Christianity has usually emphasized more the first and Islam the second aspect. Therefore, there is no celibacy in Islam and people are encouraged to marry to the extent that the Blessed Prophet said, "Marriage is half of religion." Islam accepted the positive aspect of sexuality while legislating strictly for all sexual practices and opposing and punishing severely any sexual activity outside the tenets of the Divine Law or *Sharī'ah*.

As for polygamy, there is nothing particularly moral or immoral in its practice in itself unless it is considered in the light of the laws of the society in which it is practiced. It is the breaking of religious and traditional laws of each religion and community which determines transgression and not imposing the values of one society upon another. Polygamy was practiced widely in the ancient world and of course even among Jews and Christians. Some of the Hebrew prophets had hundreds of wives. In warrior-like societies where many males died and in closely knit agricultural communities where the family worked on the land together, polygamy had a major role to play in integrating the family and the society. It prevented prostitution and unlawful sexual relations to a large extent and it had important economic consequences. Islam by permitting but legislating strict conditions for polygamy helped in practice to strengthen family bonds in the sense of integrating nearly all women into a family structure and also in stabilizing society.

In any case as far as the multiple marriages of the Blessed Prophet are concerned, they were certainly not for sensual pleasure. He did not marry until he was twenty-five and then during all the years when the sexual passions are strongest in the male, he lived with one wife who was fifteen years older than he. Moreover, his later marriages were usually for political and social reasons. They were means of bringing the various tribes of Arabia into the fold of Islam and of unifying the area which was to serve as the heartland of the new religion of Islam. If the Blessed Prophet had contracted marriages just for sensual pleasure, as so many adverse Western biographers have written, surely he would have married many women when he himself was young and at the prime of manhood and also chosen all of his wives from among young women. But a study of his life reveals very different facts.

According to the Noble Quran, Muslims are allowed to marry up to four wives if they deal with them justly and if they have the means. The Blessed Prophet was allowed more than four and in fact had up to nine wives. This was a special privilege given by God to His last Prophet. It is a kind of mystery in his life which has many meanings. Besides its political and social implication, that is, in allowing the Blessed Prophet to integrate a larger number of tribes into the Islamic community, the fact also means that although the Blessed Prophet was like other men, he was not just another man but a special being in the eyes of God. He was not an incarnation or a supernatural being but a man according to his own saying, "I am a man (*bashar*) just like you." But he was no ordinary man. According to the famous Arabic poem, "Muḥammad is a man among men as a jewel among stones." This difference between the "jewel" and the "stone" is reflected in the special privilege accorded by God to His last Prophet to marry a larger number of wives than that which Islamic Law permits to all other Muslim men. But of course "privilege" also means responsibility as the Western adage *noblesse oblige* reflects. The Blessed Prophet carried a burden of responsibility which would be inconceivable for even an exceptionally gifted human being. The "privilege" was a symbol of his pre-eminence in the human order not only from the point of view of privilege but also responsibility just like marriage itself which is at once a source of pleasure and joy and responsibility and hardship.

During the years just preceding the descent of the revelation, the future Prophet of Islam was not only occupied with the affairs of Khadījah, but was also engaged more and more in the activities of the Makkan community. Gradually he became well known and gained stature as an outstanding member of Makkan society, a person who was respected for both his capability and sense of honesty and justice. An indication of his respected position is that when he was thirty-five years old, he was asked by the people of Makkah to raise the sacred stone of the Ka'bah which was rebuilt at that time. If he had asked the members of any particular tribe to help raise the stone, other tribes would have objected and feuds would have broken out between the various tribes. It was a sign of the wisdom and statesmanship of the person through whom the Noble Quran was to be revealed shortly, that he had the stone placed in a piece of cloth and then asked members of all the tribes to lift the cloth together. In this way all the tribes shared in this singular honor of putting the sacred stone in its place.

4 The Beginning of the Revelation

At the age of forty, Muḥammad—upon whom be peace—was chosen as prophet by God. On one of the occasions when he used to retire from the city of Makkah to meditate in the mountains, the revelation descended upon him. He was in the cave of Ḥirā' on Jabal al-nūr, the "Mountain of Light," when the revelation appeared in his heart. He also had a vision of the archangel of revelation Gabriel covering the vastness of the horizon. The experience of the revelation was visual and auditory. The archangel commanded the Blessed Prophet to recite with the utterance *iqra'* which is the Arabic imperative form of recite (or read). And hence the first chapter (*sūrah*) of the Noble Quran (The Clot—XCVI) was revealed to mankind:

In the Name of God, the Beneficent, the Merciful
Read: In the name of thy Lord who createth,
Createth the human being from a clot.
Read: And thy Lord is the Most Bounteous, Who teacheth by the pen,
Teacheth the human being that which he knew not.

The first words of God revealed to the human being concerned knowledge, for Islam is essentially a religion based on the knowledge of God who is the Truth (al-Haqq) and on the distinction between Truth and falsehood.

This first experience of the revelation was so overwhelming that it overcame the Blessed Prophet completely, both psychologically and physically. It was also accompanied by the certitude that the instrument of the revelation was an angel from heaven and not a psychic force or jinn who often inspired Arab poets and seers. The revelation reverberated throughout the cosmos and the sky and transformed the whole atmosphere around the Blessed Prophet. It struck him as if with a blow and he heard loud noises and a sound like that of bells. For twenty-three years until his death, whenever the revelation came to him, the Blessed Prophet would feel that great pressure upon him. He would perspire and if he were on camel back or horseback the legs of the animal would bend under the pressure of the Word descending from above. Later the Blessed Prophet was to say, "I never receive a revelation without the consciousness which comprises my soul being taken away from me."

It is important to explain here the fundamental Islamic teaching that the Blessed Prophet was unlettered (*ummī*). How could a man who is unlettered utter the most eloquent work of the Arabic language? To understand this fundamental doctrine, it is essential to remember that the revelation was not a product of the Blessed Prophet's mind but that it descended from heaven to him. The Noble Quran is not the words of the Blessed Prophet but of God, words for which he was only the channel. The unlettered character of the Blessed Prophet means that before the Divine Message can be received, the human receptacle must be pure and clear. God does not write on simply any tablet. It required the purity of heart, soul and mind of the

Blessed Prophet untainted by human learning to serve as the tablet upon which the Divine Word was inscribed. If one understands the meaning of revelation and the complete transcendence of the Divine above all that is human and also the complementarity of the Divine Act and the human recipient, one understands why the Blessed Prophet could not but be unlettered. No amount of criticism by modern Western scholars concerning this point is of any value because they refuse to accept the reality of revelation and the difference in the level of being between the Divine Word and its human receptacle.

The Blessed Prophet descended from the mountain after the first revelation in great fear and it was only the encouragement of Khadījah that comforted him and gave him assurance. The great moment of trial was the period between the first and second instance of revelation when the Blessed Prophet was faced with some doubt as to the nature of the experience he had undergone. But with the second appearance of the archangel, he was fully assured that he had indeed been chosen as the Prophet of God.

The first person to have accepted the call of Islam was Khadījah followed by 'Alī, who was then a young boy, then Abu Bakr, Zayd, his adopted child, 'Uthmān, Talhah and Zubayr. The first visit of Gabriel to the Blessed Prophet resulted immediately in the establishment of the first nucleus of the Islamic community, a nucleus which was extremely small but which was to grow soon into a new religious community that was to expand miraculously over most of the known world of that time with lightning speed.

The years at Makkah were the heroic period of the Islamic community when it was persecuted continuously and suffered from every form of pressure. At first the followers of the Blessed Prophet were ostracized but later the injunctions against them were lifted. Nevertheless the community was persecuted to the extent that some of the

Muslims families were sent to Abyssinia where they were given refuge by the Christian king. When he was fifty years old, the Blessed Prophet experienced the bleakest period of his life. His wife Khadījah died after twenty-five years of marriage with him. The loss was almost unbearable at the beginning and practically nothing could console him. A few weeks later his uncle Abū Ṭalib also died leaving the Blessed Prophet without his most powerful protector. A short time later he married Sawdah and became betrothed also to the daughter of Abū Bakr, 'Ā'ishah, who was then only seven years old and whom the Blessed Prophet was to marry when she came of age.

During this most difficult period during which Muslims were prevented from praying and were openly molested, the Blessed Prophet enjoyed at least the support of his immediate Hāshimite family, but he was opposed by some powerful figures such as Abu Lahab and his wife who displayed open enmity toward him. Although the Hāshimites were able to protect his life, his family's support was not sufficient to prevent the opposition of the Makkan community to him from showing itself in numerous ways. The Blessed Prophet even encountered severe opposition when he tried to teach and preach in Ṭā'if and was forced to leave the city because of violent reactions against him.

The rest of the Quraysh increased their opposition and became more angered against the Blessed Prophet to the extent that he succeeded in drawing more people to his cause and persisted in his views. Obviously nothing could be more dangerous to the position of the Quraysh than a new religion based on the transcendent God and not on the idols contained in the Ka'bah. The Quraysh held a position of pre-eminence because of their control of the Ka'bah in which the idols of all the tribes of Arabia were kept. That is why they saw in the preaching of the Blessed Prophet, based on severe opposition to all idol worship, not only a religious threat but a political and social one as well. They knew fully well that if he were to succeed, Muḥammad—upon whom be peace—would create a religious and social order in which the Quraysh would no longer enjoy the economic and social privileges they held in the Makkan society of that day. Therefore, they tried in every possible way to stop the Blessed Prophet from preaching, including not only molesting him and his followers, but also offering him the rulership of Makkah if only he were to preserve the ancestral religion. But neither threat nor temptation could sway the Blessed Prophet from the mission for which God had chosen him. He persisted through every possible form of intimidation which was finally to lead to his life being threatened and his migration which transformed the history of the young Islamic community and soon the history of the world.

5 The Nocturnal Ascent

An event of singular importance occurred during the last years of the Blessed Prophet's stay in Makkah which has left its imprint upon the whole religious life of Islam and which is difficult to understand for those whose world has become limited to the physical dimension of reality. This event is the nocturnal ascent to heaven and finally to the presence of God Himself. During the month of Rajab, probably the 27th, the Blessed Prophet was taken miraculously from Makkah to Jerusalem and from there performed the *mi'rāj* or ascent through all the grades of existence to the outermost region of the cosmos, the "Lote of the Extreme Boundary" (*al-sidrat al-muntahā*) and even beyond that to the immediate proximity of God described as the station of the "distance of two bows" (*qāb al-qawsayn*). He rode upon the mythical horse *burāq* and was guided by the archangel Gabriel. The Noble Quran refers to this night journey when it says, "*Glorified be He Who carried His servant by night from the Inviolable Place of Worship [Makkah] to the Far Distant Place of Worship [Jerusalem] the neighborhood whereof We have blessed, that We might show him of Our tokens! Lo! He, only He, is the Hearer, the Seer*" (Quran—XVII:1).

This powerful, central spiritual experience of the Blessed Prophet is the example of spiritual ascent and the model for the spiritual life. The "night of ascent" (*laylat al-mi'rāj*) is the counterpart of the "night of power" (*laylat al-qadr*) when the Noble Quran was revealed during the last part of the holy month of Ramaḍān. The experience of the Blessed Prophet on the *mi'rāj* is the source of numerous masterpieces of Islamic literature including works by Ibn 'Arabi and Sana'i which even influenced European literature especially the *Divine Comedy* of Dante that is also based on the idea of ascent to heaven. The *mi'rāj* has served as a source of inspiration for generations of Muslim saints and mystics and has delineated the Islamic cosmos. Also it is the inner experiences undergone by the Blessed Prophet during the *mi'rāj* which are said to be reflected in the movements and litanies of the daily prayers, the *ṣalāt* or *namāz* that is the central and most fundamental rite of Islam.

The Noble Quran instructs Muslims to pray but the actual form of the prayer is based on the practice or *Sunnah* of the Blessed Prophet and is related to his *mi'rāj* That is also why he said, "The daily prayers are the *mi'rāj* of the faithful." According to traditional Islamic sources, however, all Muslims are able to experience *mi'rāj* spiritually (*rūḥānī*) whereas in the case of the Blessed Prophet and only in his case was the *mi'rāj* not only spiritual but also corporeal (*jismānī*). To understand the meaning of this profound assertion and also its truth, it is necessary to turn to the traditional accounts of the *mi'rāj* and understand the meaning of the traditional cosmos in which the *mi'rāj* took place. This effort in turn necessitates answering certain objections made by some modern critics blinded by the successes of modern science on the physical plane and a kind of totalitarianism which converts, often unconsciously, a science of a particular plane of reality to the science of the whole of reality thereby impoverishing that reality to an extent that it becomes subhuman.

Here is a brief summary of one of the traditional accounts of the *mi'rāj* as contained in the *Ḥayāt al-qulūb,* long popular among the Muslims of the subcontinent of India and Persia. After giving an account of his journey from Makkah to Jerusalem the Blessed Prophet says,

> Gabriel now conducted me to the first heaven. There I saw Ismā'īl, the angelic agent of that abode, and the lord of the meteors with which the demons are repelled from the heavenly mansions. There are seventy thousand angelic beings under the orders of Ismā'īl, each angelic being in turn commanding seventy thousand angels. Isma'il asked Gabriel, 'Who is this with you?' My guide replied, 'Muḥammad.' 'Has he appeared?' 'Yes,' answered the guide. Then Ismā'īl opened the gate of heaven and we exchanged greetings with each other and asked for divine blessings upon each other. He said, 'Hail and welcome, my worthy brother and prophet!' The angels drew nigh towards me and all those who saw me laughed with joy.
>
> At length I met an angelic being more immense than anything I had ever seen before. He had an ugly look and signs of anger upon his face. He also asked for my benediction like others but did not smile like them. I asked Gabriel who he was for I was fearful of him. My guide replied, 'You have cause to fear him; we also stand he awe of him. He is the overseer of hell and has never smiled since the All-powerful Lord made him the ruler of that dreadful world. His wrath against the enemies of God and against sinners who violate the Divine Law is always on the increase, and through him God takes vengeance upon them . . . (based on the translation of J. L. Merrick, *The Life and Religion of Mohammed*, Boston, 1850).

In this way the Blessed Prophet passed from one level

of being to another, passing from the infernal states through the various paradises each dominated by a prophet and a host of angels to the seventh heaven and beyond that to the *bayt al-maʿmūr* (Frequented Temple of God) where he performed two units (*rakʿah*s) of prayer. He saw the tree of paradise, the *Shajarat al-ṭūbā* then passed on to the "Lote of the Extreme Limit" (*sidrat al-muntahā*) and finally to the Divine Presence itself.

The final stage in the journey of the Blessed Prophet is described by al-Suyūṭī in his *al-Laʿālī al-maṣnūʿah* as follows:

Now when I was brought on my Night Journey to the [place of the] Throne and drew near to it, a green *rafraf* (narrow piece of silk brocade) was let down to me, a thing too beautiful for me to describe to you, whereat Gabriel advanced and seated me on it. Then he had to withdraw from me, placing his hands over his eyes, fearing lest his sight be destroyed by the scintillating light of the Throne, and he began to weep aloud, uttering *tasbīḥ, taḥmīd* and *tathniyah* (praises) to God. By God's leave, as a sign of His mercy toward me and the perfection of His favor to me, that *rafraf* floated me into the [presence of the] Lord of the Throne, a thing too stupendous for the tongue to tell of or the imagination to picture. My sight was so dazzled by it that I feared blindness. Therefore I shut my eyes, which was by God's good favor. When I thus veiled my sight God shifted my sight [from my eyes] to my heart, so with my heart I began to look at what I had been looking at with my eyes. It was a light so bright in its scintillation that I despair of ever describing to you what I saw of His majesty. Then I besought my Lord to complete His favor to me by granting me the boon of having a steadfast vision of Him with my heart. This my Lord did, giving me that favor, so I gazed at Him with my heart till it was steady and I had a steady vision of Him.

There He was, when the veil had been lifted from Him, seated on His Throne, in His dignity, His might, His glory, His exaltedness, but beyond that it is not permitted me to describe Him to you. Glory be to Him! How majestic is He! How bountiful are His works! How exalted is His position! How brilliant is His light! Then He lowered somewhat for me His dignity and drew me near to Him, which is as He has said in His book, informing you of how He would deal with me and honor me: "one possessed of strength. He stood erect when He was at the highest point of the horizon, *"Then He drew near and descended, so that He was two bows' lengths off, or even nearer"* (LIII: 6-9). This means that when He inclined to me, He drew me as near to Him as the distance between the two ends of a bow, nay, rather, nearer than the distance between the crotch of the bow and its curved ends. *"Then He revealed to His servant what he revealed"* (V:11), i.e., what matters He had decided to enjoin upon me. *"His heart did not falsify what it saw"* (V:11), i.e., my vision of Him with my heart. *"Indeed he was seeing one of the greatest signs of his Lord"* (V:18).

Now when He—glory be to Him—lowered His dignity for me He placed one of His hands between my shoulders and I felt the coldness of His fingertips for a while on my heart, whereat I experienced such a sweetness, so pleasant a perfume, so delightful a coolness, such a sense of honor in [being granted this] vision of Him, that all my terrors melted away and my fears departed from me, so my heart became tranquil. Then was I filled with joy, my eyes were refreshed, and such delight and happiness took hold of me that I began to bend and sway to right and left like one overtaken by slumber. Indeed, it seemed to me as though everyone in heaven and earth had died, for I heard no voices of angels, nor during the vision of my Lord did I see any dark bodies. My Lord left me there such time as He willed, then brought me back to my senses, and it was as though I had been asleep and had awakened. My mind returned to me and I was tranquil, realizing where I was and how I was enjoying surpassing favor and being shown manifest preference.

Then my Lord, glorified and praised be He, spoke to me, saying: 'O Muḥammad, do you know about what the Highest Council is disputing?' I answered: 'O Lord, I Thou knowest best about that, as about all things, for Thou are the One who knows the unseen' (cf. V:109/108). 'They are disputing,' He said, 'about the degrees (*darajāt*) and the excellences (*ḥasanāt*). Do you know, O Muḥammad, what the degrees and the excellences are?' 'Thou, O Lord,' I answered, 'knowest better and art more wise.' Then He said, 'The degrees are concerned with performing one's ablutions at times when that is disagreeable, walking on foot to religious assemblies, watching expectantly for the next hour of prayer when one time of prayer is over. As for the excellences, they consist of feeding the hungry, spreading peace, and performing the *tahajjud* prayer at night when other folk are sleeping.' Never have I heard anything sweeter or more pleasant than the melodious sound of His voice.

Such was the sweetness of His melodious voice that it gave me confidence, and so I spoke to Him of my need. I said: 'O Lord, Thou didst take Abraham as a friend. Thou didst speak with Moses face to face. Thou didst raise Enoch to a high place. Thou didst give Solomon a kingdom such as none after him might attain, and didst give to David the Psalter. What then is there for me, O Lord?' He replied, 'O Muḥammad, I take you as a friend just as I took Abraham as a friend. I am speaking to you just as I spoke face to face with Moses. I am giving you the *Fātiḥah* (Surah I) and the closing verses of *al-Baqarah* (II:284-286), both of which are from the treasuries of My Throne and which I have given to no prophet before you. I am sending you as a prophet to the white people of the earth and the black folk and the red folk, to *jinn* and to men thereon, though never before you have I sent a prophet to the whole of them. I am appointing the earth, its dry land and its sea, for you and for your community as a place for purification and for worship. I am giving your community the right to booty which I have given as provision to no community before them. I shall aid you with such terrors as will make your enemies flee before you while you are still a month's journey away. I shall send down to you the Master of all Books and the guardian of them, a Quran which "*We Ourselves have parceled out*" (XVII:106/107). I shall "*exalt your name for you*" (XCIV:4), even to the extent of conjoining it with My name, so that none of the regulations of My religion will ever be mentioned without you being mentioned along with Me.

Then, after this He communicated to me matters which I am not permitted to tell you, and when He had made His covenant with me and had left me there such time as He willed, He took His seat again upon His Throne. Glory be to Him in His majesty, His dignity, His might. Then I looked, and behold, something passed between us and a veil of light was drawn in front of Him, blazing ardently to a distance that none knows save God, and so intense that were it to be rent at any point it would burn up all God's creation. Then the green *rafraf* on which I was descended with me, gently rising and falling with me in 'Illiyūn . . . till it brought me back to Gabriel, who took me from it. Then the *rafraf* mounted up till it disappeared from my sight. (Translated by A. Jeffrey in his *Islam—Muhammad and His Religion.*)

The *mi'rāj* of the Blessed Prophet, which is so central to Islam, has become at the same time one of the most difficult elements in the teachings of Islam to understand for many young Muslims influenced by the modern scientific world view. In fact, certain modernized Muslims who want to reduce Islam to a rationalism and empty it of all its beauty and grandeur have sought to explain this central event away along rationalistic lines. Actually there is nothing at all illogical or "unscientific" about the nocturnal ascent if people only remember the limitations with which physical science begins. The difficulty is that these limitations are usually forgotten and the conditions which modern physical science sets upon itself in its study of physical reality are mistaken for conditions and limitations of reality itself. It is this reductionism which makes the *mi'rāj* as well as the ascent of Christ to heaven and so many other religious events mentioned in the Noble Quran and other Sacred Scriptures appear as "unreal" and "illusory."

Modern science claims to study physical reality and not other levels of reality such as the spiritual. Leading scientists are, in fact, the first to accept this limitation and usually protest against the over-generalization of the modern scientific view by popularizers and pseudo-philosophers. Nevertheless, the prestige of science today is such that people simply take to be unreal whatever is not accepted by the modern scientific world view. This fact constitutes the great tragedy of modern science which makes it such a destructive force despite certain positive aspects.

As far as the *miʿrāj* is concerned, it refers to a journey to the higher states of being and not simply through astronomical space. Moreover, since the spiritual is the principle of the psychic and the psychic is the principle of the physical, it is always possible for the lower level of reality to be integrated and absorbed into the higher. The ascension of the Blessed Prophet physically as well as psychologically and spiritually meant that all the elements of his being were integrated in that final experience which was the full realization of unity (*al-tawḥīd*). His corporeal ascent signifies also the nobility and dignity of the human body as created by God. There is nothing unscientific or illogical about the *miʿrāj* if one understands something of the multiple levels of the traditional universe and the limitation of all of modern science to a single level of reality, namely the physical, no matter how far it is stretched and extended. There is nothing worse than reducing the majestic events associated with the great founders of religion to harmless events of "ordinary life" in order to make them acceptable. This is so much more dangerous at a time when the so-called "ordinary life" has become for the most part trivial and emptied of the dignity and beauty which are characteristic of normal human existence.

6 The Migration

Although the *miʿrāj* was in a sense the spiritual crowning of the Blessed Prophet's life, it did not lead immediately to his success on the earthly plane. He was still molested and oppressed in every possible way in Makkah. In fact, life had become much more difficult because of the death of both Khadījah and Abū Ṭālib. As already mentioned, the Blessed Prophet tried to preach in other places, especially, Ṭā'if, but met with no success and was in fact driven away. It was at the darkest moment of his external life when all the doors seemed to have been closed, that a number of people from Yathrib which was later to be called *the* City or al-Madīnah, the City of the Blessed Prophet, made contact with him and invited him to journey to their city to settle existing disputes between various factions and to rule over them. This contact was made very secretly during the pilgrimage to Makkah in 622 (A.D.). It appeared to the Blessed Prophet, who was also the wisest of statesmen, that this contact was a sign from heaven which would make possible the survival and full establishment of the new religion. He thereby accepted the invitation and sent the members of the young Islamic community from Makkah to Medina in small groups so that they would not be detected. Finally only he, Abū Bakr and 'Alī remained. Meanwhile, the Makkans, fearful of the unbending will of the Blessed Prophet and the dangers which the success of his efforts would have for them, decided to attack the house of the messenger of God and kill him. Clearly a crucial moment in the life of the person who was to transform the life of the world had arrived.

Since God always protects His prophets while they are carrying out the function for which they have been chosen, the Blessed Prophet was also guided by Him to leave the scene of confrontation and to evade imminent danger at exactly the right moment. On the fateful night he and Abū Bakr set out for Medina while 'Alī was told to sleep in the bed of the Blessed Prophet. The enemies who had surrounded the house of Muḥammad—upon whom be blessings and peace—had decided to attack in unison and together to pierce his body so that no one person would be held responsible. When the would be assassins entered the house with swords and daggers drawn and removed the cover from the bed where they expected to find the Blessed Prophet sleeping, they found not the person whom they had prepared themselves to meet but the young 'Alī who had accepted the danger of death to save the life of the founder of Islam. In anger the attackers left the house in quest of the man whom they had planned to kill.

Meanwhile the Blessed Prophet and Abū Bakr had moved in the direction of Medina and taken refuge on the way in a cave. The Quraysh in their pursuit followed their footsteps on the sand and reached the mouth of the cave, but they did not enter because according to tradition a spider had spun a large cobweb around the mouth of the cave and a pair of doves had made a nest in front of it. Through the command of God the world of nature, which is so important to the Islamic revelation, came to participate in this crucial episode and saved the life of the Blessed Prophet and Abū Bakr because the Quraysh, seeing these natural elements, especially the cobweb, thought that no one could have entered the cave recently without disturbing the setting and so returned to Makkah after their futile search.

The story of the cave, like other major episodes in the life of the founder of Islam, is of great significance beyond its historic importance. Like the *mi'rāj* it points to a permanent reality for all later Muslims interested in the inner meaning of their religion. The cave is hidden from outside view like the heart of human beings and, in fact, symbolizes the heart. If one is the real friend of God, one must enter the heart where one is protected from all external dangers as were the Blessed Prophet and Abū Bakr. As Jalāl al-Dīn Rūmī asserts in his *Dīwān-i Shams*:

Consider this breast as a cave,
    the spiritual retreat of the friend;
If thou art really the companion of the cave,
    then enter the cave, enter the cave.

Moreover, the cobweb is a symbol of the created world or the cosmos itself which at the same time veils and unveils the world of the Spirit and the Divine Presence. For these reasons, the story of the refuge of the Blessed Prophet and Abū Bakr in the cave has become a favorite theme of Islamic literature and many works in both prose and poetry, such as the verses of Rūmī, have alluded to or discussed this theme.

After the danger passed away the Blessed Prophet and Abū Bakr left the cave and with the help of provisions brought by 'Alī, who had by now also left Makkah, set out for Medina where a new chapter was to begin in the life of the new religion and in fact in the history of not only Arabia but much of the world. This migration of the early Islamic community, including the founder himself from Makkah to Medina, was so important in the destiny of the new religion that the official religious calendar of Islam begins with this event which is called migration or *hijrah*. The Islamic calendar to this day is the *hijrī* calendar, having its origin in the migration of the Blessed Prophet and his followers to Medina and the establishment of the first full-fledged Islamic community in that city. It is not based, as are certain other religious calendars, such as the Christian, on the date of birth of the founder of the religion. This fact in itself shows the central importance of the event of the migration of the Blessed Prophet to Medina to the unfolding of his mission and the destiny of Islam as a religion and human community.

The migration to Medina was the beginning of a new phase in the life of the Blessed Prophet as leader of a human society and a person immersed in the life of action. It is important to note that this phase followed upon the earlier one which was more limited in scope from an external point of view but of the most intense spiritual character. It is essential to remember that the Blessed Prophet first experienced the *mi'rāj* and proximity to the Divine Presence and then migrated to Medina. The fact that the *mi'rāj* belongs to the Makkan period and that the role and function of the Blessed Prophet, as the full-fledged leader of a human community with all that such a function implies, came only later, proves the primacy of contemplation over action, of being over doing. Like all the prophets of God, the Blessed Prophet was first chosen, tested, molded and perfected and only then sent to reform and remake the world. When in Medina, he molded a human collectivity according to the Divine Will because he himself lived inwardly and outwardly according to that Will. The contour of his life is perfect proof in the Islamic context of the universal principle that in order to do good one must be good; in order to conquer the world one must first conquer oneself which means one's lower passions.

This universal truth needs to be reasserted today more than ever before when so many wish to reform the world without having reformed themselves. They want to emulate the Blessed Prophet's actions in Medina without trying to experience that spiritual ascension whose supreme example is the *mi'rāj* They wish to impose the external laws and regulations of Islam, which in itself is a very laudable act, but without uplifting themselves and the community spiritually and morally. They face thereby one impasse after another and often confront disaster as the history of the modern world, including the Islamic, reveals.

Perhaps the greatest lesson which the life of the Blessed Prophet offers for those Muslims who wish to apply the teachings of Islam to the external world about them, is that the Blessed Prophet became ruler, military leader and judge of a human community *after* and *not before* having ascended all the levels of existence and tasted the fruit of spiritual union. Of course, in the case of a prophet, there is no question of gradual self-perfection and reform. He is chosen from on high and perfected by God through angelic powers and agencies. His case differs from that of ordinary men who can in fact perfect themselves only with the help of the example of a prophet. But where the life of the Blessed Prophet provides a lesson, and an absolutely essential one, for Muslims is that inner perfection precedes outward action if that action is to be carried out according to the Truth. If a Muslim must act sincerely (with *ikhlāṣ*) and if from the Islamic point of view there is no activity without Truth, then he who acts must have first experienced the Truth and come to live accordingly.

The trajectory of the life of the person considered by Muslims as the most perfect of all of God's creatures is a dazzling example of this fundamental truth.

7 His Life in Medina

The Blessed Prophet entered Yathrib, which was to become known as *Madīnah al-nabī* or simply, al-Madinah later, on the 12th of Rabīʿ al-Awwal of the year 1 (A.H.) corresponding to September 24, 622. At that time the city was deeply divided. There were the two local tribes of Aws and Khazraj which has been carrying out a feud for generations. There was still a Jewish community which at first made peace but later caused problems for the Blessed Prophet. There were also the immigrants from Makkah called the *muhājirūn* (literally, those who migrated) and who were contrasted with those who helped the Blessed Prophet in Medina, the *anṣār* (literally, those who helped to bring about victory). The Blessed Prophet had to create a new religious community and to integrate these disparate elements into a unified society based on the principles of Islam. He had to face religious opposition not only from the Arabs but even from Jews and Christians who refused to accept his prophetic mission, rebellion from certain members of the community who had become only nominally Muslim and constant danger from the outside, especially from the Makkans who feared his new position and sought to destroy him before he could consolidate the new Islamic community. But most of all the Blessed Prophet suffered from those Medinese and *muhājirūn* who were half-hearted in their religion and whom the Noble Quran calls the *munāfiqūn*.

The Blessed Prophet was, moreover, confronted with a people whose allegiance until that time had been completely to their own tribe and not to a central authority. He was faced with a society in which centrifugal forces reigned supreme and where nothing short of a Divine intervention in human history— which in fact revelation is—could establish order and unity.

The Blessed Prophet faced these incredibly difficult obstacles with meager means. Yet, during this very time, the Noble Quran revealed to the world the fact that he was the "Seal of Prophecy" ("*he is the messenger of God and the Seal of the Prophets*," (XXXIII:40)) and the prophet whose coming was prophesied by Christ, ("*And when Jesus son of Mary said: O children of Israel! Lo! I am the messenger of God unto you, confirming that which was (revealed) before me in the Torah, and bringing good tidings of a messenger who cometh after me, whose name is the Praised One* [Aḥmad]" (LXI:6). God exalted his rank among the prophets and also gave him victory in this world to the extent that the small community established in a little town called Medina far away in the Arabian desert soon became the heart of an empire which was to stretch from China to France, a heart which was to remain over the ages as the model of the perfect Islamic community for Muslims wherever they might be.

The first and foremost challenge to the Blessed Prophet at the beginning was a military one. The Makkan armies, often in collaboration with tribes around the area of Medina, tried in every way possible to overcome the Medinese. In the year 2 A.H. the first major battle of

Islamic history took place, called the Battle of Badr, which has become enshrined in the minds and hearts of Muslims to this day as the most crucial battle and "holy war" (*jihād*) involving the very existence of the Islamic community. A small Muslim contingent was able to conquer a much larger and better organized Makkan army in battle outside of Medina. The old enemy of the Blessed Prophet, Abū Jahl, was killed in this battle and the uncle of the Blessed Prophet, 'Abbās, captured and brought to Medina. The victory was a direct sign from heaven for the young Islamic community. It consolidated the power of the newly born order and enabled the Blessed Prophet to sign treaties of alliance with some of the tribes around Medina and to fortify his position in that region.

Although the Battle of Badr and those which were to follow were crucial for the life of Islam and the new religious community, which was willed by God, still the Blessed Prophet called these battles the "small holy war" (*al-jihād al-aṣghar*) and when asked by some of the companions what then is the "greater holy war" (*al-jihād al-akbar*) he answered, "The battle against one's own carnal soul." This *ḥadīth* is perfect proof of the fact that Islam is not simply a religion of the sword. When a new religious order is established by God, the ground is cleared whether this be through a series of "holy wars" which sweep aside a decaying order or slow penetration into the foundations of the older structure which cause it to tumble. The first case is that of Islam and the second of Christianity. But that does not by any means imply the innate superiority of the "passive" means of penetration to the "active" one especially if one considers Islam's respect for all authentic religions wherever it went. Islam, instead of disregarding the question of war as if it did not exist, legislated for it and thereby limited it. *Jihād* did not mean the condoning of war but setting of limits upon it. The later history of the Islamic world in comparison with those of other civilizations, not least of all the Christian West, is sufficient proof of this assertion. Certainly the Islamic world has not fought any more wars than those worlds dominated by religions which oppose war completely. Moreover, the idea of total war and the destruction of a whole population did not originate from the Islamic world, to say the least.

The modern criticism of Islam and the Blessed Prophet on the ground that battles like that of Badr were fought in which the Blessed Prophet himself participated is based on complete misunderstanding of the role and function of the founder of Islam. The Blessed Prophet achieved perfection not by retiring from the world in the manner of Christ or the Buddha, but by participating in the world and transforming it as did the prophet-kings of the Old Testament such as David and Solomon. Islam could not have become an all-embracing way of life without considering also the question of war and struggle which characterize human life. Islam considers the symbolism of war in its positive sense, seeing life as a constant battle between truth and falsehood. No man can lead a life of equilibrium without a constant battle to maintain this equilibrium and to prevent the tensions and movements which characterize human life from destroying the harmony which is the result of *salām* (peace) and *islām* (submission) itself. And it was in the destiny of Islam that it was establish on earth, this harmony through a series of battles of a limited nature but of unbelievably far reaching consequences.

It is important to note that parallel with the victory of the Battle of Badr and the gradual consolidation of the power of the young Islamic community in the year 2 A.H., some of the most important institutions and practices of Islam were revealed and established. It was during this year that the direction of prayer (*qiblah*) was changed from Jerusalem to Makkah. It was also during this year that the fasting of the month of Ramaḍān was established as a major Islamic rite. Likewise, it was at this time that the rite of pilgrimage and the sacrifice on the 10th of Dhu'l-Ḥijjah was established as a major Islamic rite although the Blessed Prophet did not make the pilgrimage until several years later. It was God's will that during this crucial year, along with the first victory of Islam on the historic scene, the various components of the ritual aspects of Islam as a religion should be also revealed and put into practice by the Blessed Prophet for the first time in Medina.

The Makkans did not, of course, give up their pursuit after one defeat. Rather, they tried to take revenge for the Battle of Badr by assembling a larger army of some 3,000 men headed by Abū Ṣufyān and marched upon Medina in the year 3 A.H. Inasmuch as even in the providential spread of God's religion there must be both victory and defeat, success and tribulation characteristic of every endeavor in this world, the Muslims were to face a dangerous defeat at the site of Uḥud where the Blessed Prophet had decided to make a stand. At first the Muslims fought valiantly and were succeeding but soon their flank was attacked by the famous warrior, Khālid ibn Walīd, who was later to become one of the heroes of the early Islamic conquests. In this battle, however, he fought on the opposite side. During this attack, the Blessed Prophet was wounded and assumed by many to have been killed, but he was taken to the other side of a hill at the site of battle and beyond the location of the Makkan army. Many Muslims were killed during the battle including Ḥamzah, the uncle of the Blessed Prophet, but strangely enough the Makkans did not complete their rout of the Medinese and returned to Makkah. The Muslims, therefore, while tasting defeat and the loss of many of their men, were not destroyed. On the contrary, rallied by the Blessed Prophet and the great chivalrous leaders like 'Alī, they pursued their course with even greater determination.

The final attack upon Medina from the Makkan armies came in the year 5 A.H., when a large contingent of 19,000 men marched upon Medina with the hope of conquering it completely. This time the Blessed Prophet used a very successful military strategy following the advice of Salmān, the Persian, who had ditches dug around the city so that the battle came to be known as that of the Ditch (*al-khandaq*). While the city lay in siege with the Makkans unable to cross the ditches, the Blessed Prophet carried out a series of diplomatic maneuvers which enabled him to negotiate and make peace with a number of tribes around Medina. This act, added to the frustration of being unable to cross the ditches around the city, discouraged the Makkans who finally decided to uplift the siege and return to Makkah. In doing so they brought to a close the last act in the defensive phase of the life of Islam in Arabia. Henceforth the Muslims would become not only more than ever united but increase rapidly in number and begin an expansion which would soon include the whole of Arabia.

The experience of these dangers which threatened the whole of the Medinese community itself helped to weld together this newly established society. But the real integrating principle was of course the Islamic religion itself as applied by the Blessed Prophet to everyday life as well as problems of a religious, intellectual and even artistic nature. As ruler, judge, guide and teacher he was able to mold the various elements into a "people" in the Islamic sense, the *ummah*. By the year 6 A.H. the *ummah* had already come into being. Islamic society was already born as a distinct religious community which was soon to embrace a large segment of mankind. It was a remarkable achievement of the last Prophet of God to have been able to transform a heterogeneous population into an *ummah* in such a short time while warding off the greatest external dangers possible and also planting the seeds of spirituality in the hearts and souls of those saintly companions who were to carry the perfume of Islamic spirituality to the following generations.

Although Medina was now the established center of Islam, the attraction of Makkah remained as strong as ever especially since God had constituted pilgrimage to this ancient city of Abraham as part of the obligatory rites of the new religion. The Blessed Prophet had a profound urge to make the pilgrimage or *al-ḥajj*, and now that he had created the Islamic *ummah* in Medina and warded off external dangers from it, he decided to make the lesser pilgrimage or *'umrah* at the end of the year 6 A.H. With this purpose in mind he set out for the House of God moving with a large following to the vicinity of Makkah. The Makkans, feeling the danger at the Blessed Prophet's presence within the city, prevented him from entering the city of his birth. He was, therefore, forced to camp outside the city at a site called Hudaybiyyah. Thinking that perhaps the problem could be solved with the help of negotiation he sent 'Uthmān as his emissary to talk lo the Makkans and awaited their response.

The emissary did not, however, return immediately as expected and a major crisis was created for the Blessed Prophet and his followers. They could not retreat without a response nor could they move forward without an armed struggle for which they were ill-prepared since they had come in the spirit of making the pilgrimage. Everyone realized the critical nature of the confrontation. The companions came to the Blessed Prophet and made allegiance to him under a tree, vowing to fight for him and Islam to the very end. There was a new bond of loyalty and allegiance created between the Blessed Prophet and the infant Islamic community at this time which is very significant for the later religious history of the Islamic community. At the moment when he was preparing to make a final decision in this crisis with far-reaching consequences, the Makkans answered that they would allow the Muslims to make the *'umrah*, but only if this were delayed until next year. In a major diplomatic decision displaying remarkable statesmanship, the Blessed Prophet accepted the offer and a truce was made known as the Pact of Ḥudaybiyyah. The Muslims were allowed access to the sacred sanctuary and an immediate armed confrontation which would have had unforetold consequences for the Muslims at that particular moment and state of affairs was avoided.

From this point on, the tide of affairs turned for the Islamic community and the newly-born society began to expand rapidly outside the region of Medina. In the year 7 A.H., the Muslims fought and captured the oasis of Khaybar from a Jewish colony which was not expelled after the defeat but its members, being a "People of the Book," were treated as religious minorities who paid the religious tax. This practice, which is promulgated by the *Sharī'ah* as *jaziyah*, was to be followed throughout Islamic history whenever Muslims ruled over non-Muslims with their own revealed religion. The "People of the Book" came to be interpreted according to the conditions confronted by Muslims as not only Jews, Christians and Sabaeans but also Zoroastrians and later Hindus, Buddhists and others. The principle of the universality of revelation stated in the Noble Quran and the treatment of non-Muslim religious communities which possessed a revelation descended from heaven as exemplified by the treatment of the Jews by the Blessed Prophet in Khaybar, served as guiding principles for Islam as it spread throughout the world during the following centuries and confronted numerous religious communities ranging from the Chinese to those of Africa.

During the battle of Khaybar, 'Alī, who had been at the side of the Blessed Prophet throughout all moments of difficulty and scenes of crucial battles, displayed exceptional courage and bravery. He had in fact participated in every battle with the Blessed Prophet except that of Tabūk. But at Khaybar his strength, courage and fortitude in battle were such that they have become proverbial among Muslims everywhere. 'Alī had never turned his back to the enemy in any battle, but it was especially at Khaybar that his exemplary courage turned the tide and made victory for the Muslims possible. His title as the "lion of God" (*asadulallāh*) was displayed there in its full reality and more than ever before.

During the same year, as Islam began to spread further in Arabia, the Blessed Prophet turned his attention to the lands beyond and decided to invite the rulers in adjacent countries to the new religion. He sent letters to the emperors of Persia and Byzantine and the kings of Abyssinia and the Copts to accept the new religion. In a simple and majestic statement he introduced himself as the "messenger of God" (*rasūlallāh*) and invited these rulers to embrace the new religion revealed by God, *al-islām*.

It was during the year of 8 A.H. that the Blessed Prophet made the '*umrah* as stipulated by the agreement of Hudaybiyyah. After years of being away from his own city, it was a cause of great joy and satisfaction for him to be able to return to it especially since he was also performing for the first time one of the central rites of Islam. The pilgrimage itself took place in peace and quiet. Its most significant political consequence was the conversion of' several key figures of Makkah to Islam including the famous military leader and warrior, Khālid ibn Walīd, and

Amr ibn al-'Āṣ. Meanwhile many of the other important personalities such as Abū Ṣufyān, seeing the writing on the wall, began to plan secretly to join the cause of Islam without losing face.

8 The Conquest of Makkah and the Final Years of His Life

It was finally during the Ramaḍān of 8 A.H. that the Blessed Prophet set out with a sizable army consisting of both the *anṣār* and the *muhājirūn*, as well as many Bedouins, towards Makkah. The Makkans, seeing the futility of resisting, decided to surrender. Their leader, Abū Ṣufyān, came out of the city, surrendered to the Blessed Prophet and embraced Islam. And so, this most illustrious of all the sons of Makkah, Muḥammad ibn 'Abdallāh—may peace and blessings be upon him—entered, without fighting, the city of his birth from which he had been forced to migrate. The orphan who had suffered so much as a child and was persecuted in every possible way even after being chosen by God as His prophet, now entered the city of God in full glory and as the ruler of a human community as well as a whole sector of God's creation.

Almost all the Makkans accepted Islam, and the Blessed Prophet, being the most perfect of human beings, rather than being bridled by petty human weaknesses such as the sense of revenge, accepted with magnanimity and generosity the surrender of all those who had opposed him so much until a short while before. As long as they proclaimed in their words to be Muslims, they were forgiven and accepted into the new community. He held no personal grudge nor any animosity for his goal was the establishment of a new order based on truth and justice and not personal vindictiveness or reprisal for ill deeds committed against him and his companions.

To the same extent that the Blessed Prophet forgave human beings, he was adamantly opposed to the idolatry of the pagan Arabs. His wrath turned not against individuals who asked forgiveness and embraced Islam, whether with earnestness or even through expediency, but against the idols of a crassly materialistic and individualistic nature which cluttered the House of God and hid its original purity as the abode of the Presence of the One whom no image or idol can depict or reflect. The Blessed Prophet came to the Ka'bah where he ordered all the idols to he broken and destroyed. It was 'Alī who helped most in carrying out this order by breaking the heaviest and largest of the idols named Hubal. The Blessed Prophet also had all the walls of the Ka'bah cleared of the images which had been painted upon them except for an icon of the Virgin Mary and Christ which he protected by pulling his hands on them.

This profound act symbolized not only the respect of Islam far these two figures, a respect which is reflected in many verses of the Noble Quran, but also the basic difference between an idol or graven image in the Quranic sense and a symbol associated with sacred art. The idols of Arab paganism were simply man-made statutes reflecting not a celestial reality but purely human elements. They were the idols (called *ṣanam* or *wathan*) in the Noble Quran which form the basis of the idolatry so contrary to the Islamic perspective and opposed to the spirit of the Noble

Quran. The traditional Christian images protected by the Blessed Prophet, however were painted according to the principles of sacred art and norms and methods received through angelic inspiration by St Luke. They were therefore of a totally different nature. They were not idols, but symbols reflecting a Divine Presence according to the principles and norms of another religion whose perspective allowed such religious representation. By protecting these icons, the Blessed Prophet not only underlined the difference between an idol and a sacred image, but also pointed out that although the Islamic perspective did not allow representation in its sacred art, this did not mean that representation was illegitimate in the sacred art of another religion with a different structure and perspective.

Without doubt the triumphal entry into Makkah was the highlight of the earthly life of the Blessed Prophet and crowned years of suffering and incessant struggle to establish God's religion on earth. It was a moment of exaltation which also revealed most fully the nobility of the soul of the Blessed Prophet with all his generosity and magnanimity.

The Noble Quran reflects the grandeur of this moment in these verses:

In the Name of God, the Beneficent, the Merciful
When God's succor, and the triumph cometh
And thou seest mankind entering the religion of God in troops,
Then hymn the praise of thy Lord, and seek forgiveness of Him. Lo! He is ever ready to show mercy. (CX)

And it is most of all in reference to the victory at Makkah, which is also the climax of the victory of Islam itself, that the Noble Quran states, "*Lo! We have given thee (O Muḥammad) a signal victory that God may forgive thee of thy sin that which is past and that which is to come, and may perfect His favor unto Thee, and may guide thee on a right path. And that God may help thee with strong help*" (XLVIII:1-3).

The victorious entry into Makkah was also the key to the domination of Islam over the whole of Arabia. After settling affairs in Makkah, the Blessed Prophet faced the Ḥawāzin tribe in Central Arabia at Hunayn. A dangerous battle was fought which the Muslims won only with great difficulty. Then he marched upon Ṭā'if which because of its fortified walls offered stiff resistance. In fact it was the change of heart of the inhabitants that finally brought the city to the Islamic side. Realizing the truth of the new heavenly message and the victory which accompanied it, the people of Ṭā'if adopted Islam and surrendered of their own accord. In this way the major cities of Arabia all embraced the new faith. The Medinese in fact became apprehensive, fearing that with Makkah and Ṭā'if in Muslim hands, the Blessed Prophet would leave Medina and make his city of birth the capital of Islam. But such was not to be the case. After these conquests the Blessed Prophet allayed the fears of the *anṣār* and returned to Medina which was now fast becoming the capital of Arabia, both religiously and politically.

In the year 9 A.H., the aim of the Blessed Prophet to unite the whole of Arabia under the banner of Islam took a major step forward when many emissaries came from tribes all over the Arabian peninsula to accept Islam and pay allegiance to God's last Prophet. Meanwhile, the decision was made to bring northern Arabia also under the sway of Islam and to redeem the losses suffered earlier by Muslims in this region. The Blessed Prophet himself led the march to Tabūk where the Muslim armies met with success. In fact the prestige of Islam had risen so greatly that some of the local Christian and Jewish rulers in the region submitted to the Blessed Prophet. This victory in the north was particularly important since at this moment there were certain dissident forces in Medina and the centrifugal tendencies of Arabian society were pulling against the unity created by the new religion.

Parallel with northern Arabia, southern Arabia including Yemen, 'Umān and Baḥrayn fell under the sway of Islam and became fully Muslims during the lifetime of the Blessed Prophet. This region had been under strong Persian influence and in fact probably the first Persian converts to Islam— excluding the famous Salmān al-Fārsī—came from this region. What is particularly interesting is that this region, especially Yemen, embraced Islam without any conquests by Muslim armies. The great Yemeni saint Uways al-Qaranī had heard about the Prophet of God and embraced his call without even seeing him. He had come to love the Blessed Prophet from afar with a love which has symbolized for generations of Islamic mystics the love of the man of God for his Creator and initiation into the Divine Mysteries from afar. The Uwaysīs to this day form a particular branch of Sufism based on initiation by the mysterious green turbaned prophet Khaḍir or Khiḍr rather than a regular human spiritual master.

As for Salmān al-Fārsī, he, too, became a great saint of early Islam and, in fact, like Uways joined 'Alī later when the latter became caliph. Salmān was the first Persian to embrace Islam as Bilāl, the person who called the people to prayer during the lifetime of the Blessed Prophet, was the first Black to become Muslim. Both men were loved dearly by the founder of Islam and were like members of his family. Their presence symbolizes the rapid spread of

Islam among the Persians and the Blacks. In fact after the Arabs, it was the Persians and Blacks who accepted Islam in great numbers before other major ethnic groups such as the Turks, Indians and Malays.

With the spread of Islam to northern and southern Arabia, the vision of the Blessed Prophet to unify Arabia through Islam and to create a society based on justice and virtue was realized. The Blessed Prophet was able to unite warring tribes, the rich and poor, the powerful and the meek into a society in which distinction was based upon nobility of soul and piety. He was able to actualize on earth the truth contained in this verse of the Noble Quran, *O mankind! Lo! We have created you male and female, and have made you nations and tribes that ye may know one another Lo! the noblest of you, in the sight of God, is the best in conduct. Lo! God is Knower, Aware* (XLIX; 13).

Towards the end of the year 10 A.H., the Blessed Prophet decided to make the first completely Islamic pilgrimage to Makkah, one in which only Muslims would be present at the House of God and its precinct according to the practice which has been followed ever since. This pilgrimage which instituted the *ḥajj* as a purely Islamic institution was also destined to be the "Farewell Pilgrimage." It marked the final achievement of the unparalleled career of God's most perfect creature. The essence of the unforgettable sermon of the Blessed Prophet on this occasion, which has echoed through the hearts and minds of Muslims over the ages, is contained in these famous Quranic verses which have also given the name of Islam to the religion brought by Muḥammad ibn 'Abdallāh—may peace and blessings be upon him. "*This day are those who disbelieve in despair of (ever harming) your religion; so fear them not, fear Me! This day have I perfected your religion for you and completed My favor unto you, and have chosen for you as religion AL-ISLAM*" (V:3).

The orations delivered by the Blessed Prophet during this "Farewell Pilgrimage" were all of great eloquence and beauty summarizing the teachings of Islam and his own *Sunnah* which he was to bequeath to the Islamic community. Here is perhaps the most memorable of the orations delivered on the 9th of Dhu'l-Ḥijjah in the year 10 A.H. near the end of the ceremonies of the "Farewell Pilgrimage" at 'Arafāt:

All praise is for God. We praise Him; seek His help and pardon; and we turn to Him. We take refuge with God from the evils of ourselves and from the evil consequences of our actions. There is none to lead him astray whom God guideth aright and there is none to guide him aright whom He misguideth. I bear witness that there is no god but God, alone without any partner, and I bear witness that Muḥammad is His slave and His Apostle. I admonish you, O slaves of God, to fear God and I urge you to be obedient to him and I open the speech with that which is good.

Now to proceed, O people, listen to me; I will deliver a message to you. For I do not know whether I shall ever have an opportunity to meet you after this year in this place. O people verily your blood (lives), your properties and your honor are sacred and inviolable to you till you appear before your Lord, like the sacredness of this day of yours, in this city of yours. Verily, you will meet your Lord and He will ask you about your actions. Lo, have I conveyed the message? O God, bear witness. So he who bears with himself any trust, should restore it to the person who deposited it with him. Be aware; no one committing a crime is responsible for it but himself. Neither son is responsible for the crime of his father nor father is responsible for the crime of his son.

Lo, O people, listen to my words and understand them. You must know that the Muslim is the brother of the Muslim and the Muslims are one brotherhood. Nothing belonging to his brother is lawful for a Muslim except what he himself allows. So you should not oppress yourselves. O God, have I conveyed the message? Behold, everything of Ignorance is put down under my two feet. The blood-revenges of the Age of Ignorance are remitted. Verily, the first blood-revenge I cancel is the blood-revenge of Ibn Rabī'ah ibn Ḥārith who was nursed in the tribe of Sa'd and whom the Hudhail killed. The interest of the Age of Ignorance period is abolished. But you will receive your capital-stock. Do not oppress and you will not be oppressed. God has decreed that there is no interest. The first interest which I cancel is that of 'Abbās ibn 'Abd al-Muṭṭalib. Verily it is canceled entirely.

O people, do fear God concerning women. you have taken them with the trust of God and you have made their private parts lawful with the word of God. Verily you have received certain rights over your women and your women have certain rights over you. Your right over them is that they should not make anybody, whom you dislike, trample down your beds, and that they should not allow anyone whom you dislike (to enter) into your house. If they perform such an action, then God has permitted you to harass them keep them separate in their beds and beat them but not severely. If they refrain they must have their sustenance and clothing justly from you.

Behold, receive with kindness the recommendation given about women. For they are middle-aged women (or helpers) with you. They do not possess anything for themselves and you cannot have from them more than that. If they obey you in this way, then you should not treat them unjustly. Lo, have I conveyed? O God, be witness.

O people, listen and obey though a mangled Abyssinian slave becomes your ruler who executes the Book of God among you. O people, verily God appropriated to everyone his due. No will is valid for an inheritor and a will is not lawful for more than one-third (of the property).

The child belongs to the (legal) bed and for the adulterer there is stoning. He who relates (his genealogy) to other than his father or claims his client ship to other than his master, the curse of God, the angels and the people—all these—be upon him. God will accept from him neither repentance nor righteousness.

O people, verily Satan is disappointed from being ever worshipped in this land of yours. But he is satisfied to be obeyed in other matters that you think very trifling of your actions. So be cautious of him in your religion. Verily, I have left behind among you that which if you catch hold of you will never be misled later on—a conspicuous thing, i.e., the Book of God and sunnah of His Apostle.

O people, Gabriel came to me, conveyed salad from my Lord and said, 'Verily God, the Mighty and the Great, has forgiven the people of 'Arafāt and the Sanctuary (to forego) their shortcomings'."

'Umar ibn al-Khaṭṭāb stood up and said, 'O Apostle of God, is it for us only?' He replied, 'It is for you and for those who are to come after you till the Day of Resurrection.'

And you will be asked about me, then what would you say? They replied, 'We bear witness that you have conveyed the message, discharged (your duty) and admonished.'

Then he said, raising his ring-finger towards heaven and pointing it out towards the people, 'O God, bear witness; O God, bear witness; O God, bear witness.' (from Maulana M. Ubaidul Akbar, *The Orations of Muhammad*, Lahore, 1954, pp. 79-78 [with certain modifications]).

It was upon returning from Makkah to Medina that a major incident took place at Ghadir Khumm near a pool of water, an incident which has influenced the history of Islam to this day. It was at this site that, according to one group of Muslims called the "partisans of 'Alī" (*shī'at al-'Alī*) and later known as Shi'ites or Shi'ah, the Blessed Prophet chose 'Alī as his successor and inheritor. The Sunni sources also allude to the event of Ghadīr Khumm, but naturally interpret it in a different manner. For them the praise of 'Alī by the Blessed Prophet even as his "inheritor" did not mean political succession as Sunni jurists were later to understand the issue. In any case, this incident is the historical event which symbolizes and also crystallizes the different perspectives of Sunnism and Shiʿism even within the lifetime of the Blessed Prophet and in a sense externalizes what existed already within the soul of the founder of the religion. For surely these two major interpretations of Islam, both orthodox and placed by the hands of Providence within the Islamic revelation to integrate different mentalities and types into the unitary perspective of Islam, reflect two dimensions within the soul of the Blessed Prophet and were reflected in his closest companions.

No religion which is destined to comprehend many nations and peoples can be bound by just one interpretation, uniformity is not unity but its antithesis. Despite all the historical struggles and tensions, the unity of Islam was no more destroyed by the Sunni-Shiʿite divergence than it was by the four Sunni schools of law. This unity is threatened today, however, by the intrusion of modernism in all its forms, including religious fanaticism according to alien models, and the manipulation of Sunni-Shiʿite differences by international political forces and not by the interpretations of Ghadīr Khumm which marks the external crystallization of Sunni-Shiʿite distinctions which only externalized at the providential moment what was bound to manifest itself through the course of Islamic history.

In any case here is the account of Ghadīr Khumm and the famous oration of the Blessed Prophet according to a traditional Shiʿite source,

> When the ceremonies of the pilgrimage were completed, the Prophet, attended by ʿAlī and the Muslims, left for Makkah. Before reaching Medina he halted, although that place had never before been a stopping-place for caravans, because it had neither water nor pasturage. The reason for encamping in such a place was that illustrious verses of the Quran came powerfully upon him, enjoining him to establish ʿAlī in the caliphate. He

had previously received communications to the same effect, but not expressly appointing the time for 'Alī's inaugurations which, therefore, he had deferred lest opposition should be excited and some forsake the faith. If the company of pilgrims had passed Ghadīr Khumm, they would then have dispersed to their several quarters; therefore the Lord of the universe willed them to be assembled in this place, that all might hear what should be said to the commander of the faithful, and evidence in the case be complete, and no Muslim have any excuse for not acquiescing in the appointment.

This was the message from the Most High, 'O apostle, publish the whole of that which hath been sent down unto thee from thy Lord: for if thou do not, thou dost not in effect publish any part thereof; and God will defend thee against wicked men, for God directeth not the unbelieving people.' Being thus peremptorily commanded to appoint 'Alī his successor and threatened with penalty if he delayed when God had become his surety, therefore the Prophet halted in this unusual place, and the Muslims dismounted around him.

As the day was very hot, he ordered them to take shelter finder some thorn trees. Having ordered all the camel-saddles to be piled up for a member or rostrum, he commanded his herald to summon the people around him. Most of them had bound their cloaks on their feet as a protection from the excessive heat. When all the people were assembled, the Prophet ascended the member of saddles, and calling up to him the commander of the faithful, placed him on his right side. Muḥammad—may peace and blessings on him—now rendered thanksgiving to God, and then made an eloquent address to the people, in which he foretold his own death, and said, 'I have been called to the gate of God and the time is near when I shall depart to God, be concealed from you, and bid farewell to this vain world. I leave among you the book of God, to which, while you adhere, you will never go astray. And I leave with you the members of my family who cannot be separated from the book of God till both rejoin me at the fountain of Kawthar.' He then, with a loud voice, demanded, 'Am I not dearer to you than your own lives?' and was answered by the people in the affirmative. He then took the hands of 'Alī and raised them so high that the white of his armpits appeared, and said, 'Whoever heartily receives me as his master, then to him 'Alī is the same. O Lord, befriend every friend of 'Alī, and be the enemy of all his enemies; help those that aid him, and abandon all that desert him.'

It was now nearly noon, and the hottest part of the day, and the Prophet descended from the pulpit and performed two units of prayer by which time it was meridian. The call having been proclaimed, the Prophet and Muslims performed the noon prayers, after which he went to his tent, beside which he ordered a tent to be pitched from the commander of the faithful. When 'Alī was seated in the tent, the Blessed Prophet commanded the Muslims, company by company, to wait upon 'Alī, congratulate him on his accession to the imamate, and salute him as amir and king of the faithful. All this was done by both men and women, none appearing more joyful at the inauguration of 'Alī than did 'Umar . . .

The Traditions we are now following declare that the Blessed Prophet here [in Ghadīr Khumm} ordered a pulpit of stones to be built, which he ascended and said, 'God is worthy of praise and adoration, being exalted in His own unity, and glorious in sovereignty, His greatness is manifest to all His creatures, His omniscience extends to every thing, and His omnipotence rules over all. Forever is He lord of His own greatness, and worthy of all praise and adoration. He created the high heavens and leveled the low earths. He is most holy and infinitely free from all defect, the Lord of angels and the Spirit (*rūḥ*). He is gracious to all His creatures, and bestows favors upon all whom He causes to approach the gate of his glory. He sees all eyes, but they see not him. He mercifully sustains His creatures, and is the Lord of knowledge and dignity. His mercy extends to all, and every thing is under obligation to His favor. He punishes according to justice. His vengeance does not hastily arise, and He punishes less than is deserved. He knows the secrets of all hearts, and nothing is concealed from Him. Nothing to him is secret or doubtful. He encompasses all things, and is almighty over all. Nothing resembles Him. He created all things when as yet there was nothing. He is eternal and without decline. He rules justly among men. There is no Lord besides Him. He is rightly almighty to execute whatever He declares, and all His works are in wisdom. He knows every trifling thing that is done, and is the creator of the minutest atoms. In what is visible and manifest it is impossible to describe a single part of the perfection He displays. His mode of being is unknown, and nothing is understood of His mysteries but what He reveals. I testify, by His holy nature, to mankind, that He is the Lord besides whom there is no Lord, and no other existence is worthy of worship. He has filled the world with manifestations of His holiness, purity, light and presence, and from eternity to eternity He enlightens all. He is the Lord who executes His own decrees without the counsel of any intelligent being, and has no associate in ordaining His works, and there is no contrariety in His counsels. He created all things without a model, and brought them into being without any one taking trouble concerning it. He created man from non-existence, and besides Him there is no Creator. He firmly established His works and bestowed good gifts on His creatures. He is the Just who never oppresses, and the most Merciful to whom all things return. I testify that He humbles all things before His greatness by His own terrible majesty. He is universal King, who built the heavens and guides the sun and moon for the benefit of His creatures, which luminaries shall circulate till an appointed time. He draws the curtain of night over the face of day, and the curtain of day over the face of night. He is the crusher of every enemy and the destroyer of every devil.

'There is nothing correspondent to Him or like Him. He is One, the only God of all creatures, to whom alone they can appeal in their necessities. He is neither paternal nor filial in His nature, and is not subject to accident. He is worshipped in His unity, and is the great Lord. He purposes, then performed wills, and then commands, and knows and numbers all things. He causes to die, and after death restores to life. He makes rich and makes poor. He causes to laugh and to weep. He brings near and removes far off. Sometimes He prohibits, and sometimes permits. Sovereignty is His peculiar prerogative. He is worthy of the best worship. All are in His hand, and He is almighty over all. He is victorious and forgiving, the hearer of prayer, and the great Giver of favors. He numbers the respirations, and is the Preserver of *jinns* and of mankind, and nothing is difficult or troublesome to Him, nor do the importunities of solicitors weary Him. He is the protector of the good, and bestows favors on the prosperous. He is the Lord of believers, and the Preserver of the universe; that Lord who is entitled to the praise of all His creatures, both in the time of their prosperity and in the season of their greatest calamity.

'I believe in Him, and in His angels, books, and prophets. I hear His commands, and obey them, and hasten to do whatever pleases Him, and accept whatever He pleases lo send, such is my desire to perform His mandate, and such my fear of His vengeance; for He is the Lord from whose wrath there is no refuge, though oppression is not to be apprehended from Him. I profess myself His servant. I claim Him for my protector, and communicate what He has imparted to me, in fear, if I should not, great punishment would overtake me, which none, though most skilled in stratagem, could avert, for there is no Lord besides Him. Verily, He has declared to me that if I do not perform what He has commanded, I shall be unfaithful in His apostleship; verily, He guarantees me security from human harm, and He is able to avert the mischief of all enemies. He manifests mercy to His friends.

'God, O people, has communicated to me a command which I have committed no fault in not imparting to you hitherto, and that I will now deliver to you. Three times has Gabriel visited me with a salutation from my Lord, and commanded me that I should stand in this place and declare to all, both white and black, that 'Alī ibn Abī Ṭālib is my brother, and heir, and *khalīfah*, and the leader after me. His rank and relation to me is like that of Hārūn to Mūsā, except there is no prophet after me. He is constituted over you, with authority to command, next to God and His prophet. This is the meaning of the passage which the Most High has communicated to me in the Quran, *Verily, your protector is God and his apostle, and those who believe, who observe the stated times of prayer, and give alms, and who bow down to worship* (Quran V: 60).

'I know the Most High will not be satisfied unless I perform what He has commanded. Know ye, then O people, that the Lord of the universe has ordained 'Alī your prince and ruler, your imam and leader, and has made obedience to him obligatory on the *muhājirīn* and the *anṣār*, on citizens and on inhabitants of the desert, on Arabs and Persians, on free and bond, small and great, white and black, on all who worship God in the unity of His nature. Over all these the authority of 'Alī extends and his orders reach. Whoever disobeys him is accursed, and all that render him due obedience shall enjoy the mercy of God. And whoever testifies to his truth and rights, hears and obeys him, God will pardon.

'O ye people, this is the last time I am to stand in such an assembly; then hear my words, obey my injunctions, and receive the commands of your Lord. Verily, God is master of your life and is your Creator, and next to Him His prophet Muḥammad is your lord, empowered to command, to guide your counsels and declare what is necessary. Next to me, 'Alī is your prince and leader, in following the commands of the Lord of the universe." (from the *Ḥayāt al-qulūb*, trans. by J. L. Merrick, pp. 334-339, with certain modifications by S. H. Nasr).

The Sunni version of this episode is of course not identical with the Shi'ite, but there are numerous references in Sunni *Ḥadīth* literature to the special relationship between the Blessed Prophet and 'Alī and the events of Ghadīr Khumm which have of course been interpreted in a different fashion by Sunni jurists. For example, the famous *Ḥadīth al-manzilah* in which Sa'd ibn al-Waqqāṣ recounts from the Blessed Prophet who addressed 'Alī, "Are you not satisfied to be to me what Hārūn was to Moses except that after me there will not be another Prophet?" has been seen in over a hundred versions in Sunni sources.

As for the *ḥadīth* of Ghadīr Khumm itself, such prominent sources as the *Sunans* of Ibn Mājah, al-Tirmidhī and

Aḥmad ibn Ḥanbal mention it specifically. In Ibn Mājah (*al-Muqaddimah, Bāb* 11, *ḥadīth* 116, vol. I, Cairo, 1954) in a *ḥadīth* in reference to 'Alī, the Blessed Prophet says, "And he is the *mawlā* of him for whom I am the *mawlā*." In al-Tirmidhī (*Kitāb al-manāqib, Bāb* 20, Vol. V, p. 633, Cairo, n.d.) and Aḥmad ibn Ḥanbal (Vol. I, pp. 1, 84, 118, 119, 152, 331 and Vol. IV, pp. 281, 327, and 370; and even in several other places, Beirut n.d.) the *ḥadīth* is repeated in the form of, "He for whom I am his *mawlā*, verily 'Alī is his *mawlā*."

The key question is, therefore, not the occurrence of Ghadīr Khumm or the selection before the Islamic community of 'Alī as *mawlā*, confirmed by so many Sunni and Shi'ite sources, but the meaning of the word *mawlā* which was understood in different senses by the Sunni and Shi'ite communities, respectively. The word comes from the Arabic root (*wly*) and the terms *walī* and *mawlā* appear in the Noble Quran where they have also been interpreted in different ways by various commentators. The terms derived from this root mean at once friend, ruler, master, and heir and many other key concepts which have been developed over the centuries by Islamic thinkers, the term *walāyah/wilāyah* being one of the most complex in Islamic thought. There is no doubt, therefore, that *mawlā* certainly does contain the meaning of master and heir, but whether it also means leader of the community in the political sense succeeding the Blessed Prophet or not is what was not agreed upon in his designation of 'Alī as his "successor."

Today, what is important is to create better understanding between Sunnis and Shi'ites on the basis of historical facts as understood traditionally, but with fresh interpretations in the direction of harmony between all schools of Islamic thought and with reference to the

Blessed Prophet himself in whose being, thoughts and actions all the authentic manifestations of Islam met in a unity which should serve as a point of reference and model for all generations of Muslims and especially those of today so much in need of unity. In any case, Ghadīr Khumm remains as one of the most significant moments of the life of the Prophet as far as the later history of the Islamic community is concerned.

After this momentous occasion, the Blessed Prophet returned to Medina having completed his earthly duties and therefore, although apparently in full health and in fact preparing for a campaign in the north and carrying out the affairs of state, he was called back to the Lord. He fell ill in a sudden manner, coming down with fever. After three days of serious illness he passed into the hands of his Creator on the 13th of Rabīʿ al-Awwal of the year 10 A.H. leaving behind a work which was as enduring as it was grandiose. Through the Will of God, the poor orphan in Makkah had transformed forever the whole of human history. His earthly remains were buried by ʿAlī, Fāṭimah and other members of his family in the very house in which he lived while the Medinese community was debating the future of the Islamic community in the mosque nearby. His exalted soul ascended to the highest empyrean, to the Divine Presence, to guard and protect with God's Will the last phase of the journey of the caravan of life of that major segment of humanity which has been destined to follow the religion brought by him into the world, the religion of Islam which shall last as long as men live and breath on this earth. May the blessings and peace of God be upon him who was himself mercy unto the world.

9 The Role and Character of the Blessed Prophet

In several verses of the Noble Quran such as verses XXXIV:50, XL:55, and XLVII:19, reference is made to the fact that the Prophet of Islam was human and not divine in the sense of an incarnation, but these verses do not at all negate the preeminence of the Blessed Prophet as the most perfect of human beings, as the "jewel among stones" according to the Arabic verse already cited. Otherwise how could the same Noble Quran assert that he was chosen as the best model (*uswā*) for Muslims to follow. It is because of the perfection borne by him that he has served generations of Muslims as perfect example. There is no doubt that he was given by God an eminence which is certainly not ordinary and not simply human as this word is used today although theologically he was not a divine descent but a man. There is no better proof of his extraordinary eminence than his inerrancy (*'iṣmah*), that he was protected from error by God whether this protection is understood in the particularly Shi'ite sense of his very substance having been immune to sin from the beginning or that he was "washed" and purified by the angels as the story mentioned above about his breast being washed by the angels bears out.

In any case there is no greater danger for Muslims today than that of reducing the majestic grandeur of the Blessed Prophet to petty human conditions on the outward excuse that he was merely human while in reality catering to the prevailing humanism of the modern West. The fact that the Blessed Prophet was a human being does not mean that he was ordinary like any other human being but that the human state has the possibility of the grandeur and fullness displayed by his personality and character. To contemplate the life, virtues and achievements of the Blessed Prophet is to realize not only the greatness of God's power and that of his prophets, but also the tact that mankind as a whole lives so much below the level of the really human. The prophets and saints display to mankind the total possibility of existence. It is they who elevate the meaning of "human being" to its highest norm and no greater disservice can be done to human beings than to reduce them to the petty and often trivial standards of modern man rather than holding them as everliving ideals and examples who can help human beings realize to some extent at least the total and full nature of the human state.

For generations of Muslims, before the humanism of the modern world contaminated the minds and souls of many of them, the Blessed Prophet fulfilled such a function on the highest level and he remains and will remain, as long as Islam survives as a religion, as the supreme example for human beings to follow. [The Blessed Prophet in a sense experienced the fullness of all that is human in order to be able to fulfill his function as the prophet of Islam which has penetrated every aspect of human life in order to be able to integrate all of life into the Center which sanctifies and gives meaning to all things.]

[margin note: humanity vs. divinity]

[bottom note: God let him experience this humanity in order to make the Prophet him perfect to integrate all of things, all of]

There is practically no aspect of human life which the Prophet of Islam did not experience. On the personal and human level he experienced the loss of both parents at a tender age, loneliness, social pressures, material poverty and practically every kind of ordeal a young person could undergo in society. Later in life, he was to be witness to every form of grief, the loss of his beloved wife Khadījah, the early death of sons, betrayal by members of his own tribe, constant threats to his life, property and family not to speak of continuous dangers facing the cause for which he was chosen and to which he had dedicated himself totally, namely the cause of Islam.

Since human life is woven of threads of joy and sorrow, the Prophet of Islam was also blessed with the experience of every form of joy possible to human beings starting of course with that highest joy and in fact ecstasy which is the knowledge and love of God, the supreme gift given to him as a special blessing from Heaven with a degree of exaltedness and intensity unimaginable to other human beings. But on the more ordinary level of human life, he was blessed with the joy of a very happy marriage to Khadījah, of having a daughter such as Fāṭimah who was like an angelic substance fallen upon the earth, of a cousin and son-in law like 'Alī, whose devotion to the Blessed Prophet and dedication to his call are extraordinary by whatever standards they are judged. The Blessed Prophet also had dedicated friends and disciples like Abū Bakr and Salmān and had tasted the full meaning of human as well as Divine friendship (being himself the Friend of God, (*ḥabiballāh*). He had experienced aspects of human nature from the vantage point of a poor orphan, a successful merchant, the endangered leader of a semi-clandestine community and the triumphant leader of a new society which was soon to conquer much of the world. He had sold goods to small merchants as well as written letters to the mightiest emperors and rulers on earth inviting them to the cause of Islam. He had tasted defeat as well as victory and been even blessed with the possibility of experiencing the incomparable joy of forgiving his worst enemies at the moment of his conquest of Makkah. Finally, he had tasted both failure and success. He had persevered over long years in hope and reliance upon God while being witness to bitter failures and was then destined to taste the sweetness of one success after another to the extent that he was able to realize, before his death, all that he had set out to achieve. There is surely little that a Muslim can experience and few situations he can face in human life without there being a precedent in the life of the Blessed Prophet which can always serve as model and source of inspiration and instruction for him.

As far as the basic functions in society are concerned, again the Blessed Prophet was destined by God to fill nearly all of them. He was a teacher, head of a household, merchant, statesman, political and social leader, military commander, judge and supreme ruler not to speak of his specifically prophetic functions such as bringing a Divine Law and the Word of God to mankind, instructing men in esoteric as well as exoteric knowledge, being gifted with complete insight into human nature and the psychology of human beings at different moments and on various occasions, etc.

In each of these functions he left behind a precious heritage which has become part and parcel of Islam and its culture. As a teacher the Blessed Prophet was eminently successful in imparting knowledge of various orders to very different types of people. He was in fact the supreme teacher. He was so successful in this task that today he still remains the most important and effective teacher for Muslims. His sayings and acts, his thoughts and deeds, continue to teach his community from day to night while the more intellectual and spiritual instructions imparted by him continue to form and mold the minds and souls of those members of the Islamic community who are in quest of spiritual perfection.

As the head of a household, the Blessed Prophet created a miniature society and in fact universe whose structure and internal relations are of keen interest to devout Muslims to this day. His manner of dealing with his wives, his children and the small grandchildren, that is, Hasan and Ḥusayn, his duties and functions within the house, his sense of responsibility towards the family, his inculcation of love and trust among members of the family and many other elements are parts of his *Sunnah* and elements of his character which make him an example to be emulated and followed not only as an individual but in the context of the human family. Likewise, the manner in which he acted when a merchant, or when he was judging a case or acting as military leader in the field of battle or ruling over a human community or deciding on a problem of diplomacy all reveal aspects of a being who was chosen to fulfill all the possibilities inherent in the human state. It is a sobering thought to remember that the same person who led the Battle of Badr and who later ruled over a whole segment of the universe would bend down on the floor of his humble house so that his grandchildren could mount upon his back and ride around the room. Only a prophet can achieve this perfection of grandeur and humility, power and generosity, but the fact that he can achieve it reveals how great man could be if only he knew who he is.

Of course each prophet and especially the last among them possesses all the human virtues, but in the case of each prophet a set of virtues stand out and are more emphasized, virtues which are associated with the structure of the religion brought into the world by the prophet in question. The eminent virtue of some prophets has been love and others withdrawal, fear of God and asceticism. As far as the Blessed Prophet is concerned, his eminent virtues were sincerity towards God and the Truth, generosity towards all beings and spiritual poverty associated with simplicity and humility. The Blessed Prophet has said, "Poverty is my pride" (*al-faqr*^{u} *fakhrī*) and Islamic spirituality is often called "Muḥammadan poverty" (*al-faqr al-muḥammadī*). This did not mean that the Blessed Prophet was opposed to the people who were wealthy or disdained earthly possessions. His own wife Khadījah was, after all, a wealthy merchant. What this *faqr* meant was essentially humility and awareness of our nothingness before God while preferring simplicity to ornateness and luxury. The Blessed Prophet was hard with himself and sought constantly to discipline himself. He always emphasized humility although he was the greatest of men and certainly aware of his own nature. But much of his *Sunnah* and the *adab* or manner of acting associated with it exists for the purpose of inculcating the virtue of humility (*tawāḍu'* or *khushū'*) whose highest form is our awareness of our nothingness before God, symbolized also by the prostrations during the daily prayers.

The Blessed Prophet was also full of generosity and magnanimity (*kirāmah* or *sharaf*). To the same extent that he was strict with himself, he was generous with others. Nobility of character implies both giving and forgiving, the giving of oneself and one's efforts, thoughts and belongings to others and the forgiving of the faults of others and what they have done to one's person. The Blessed Prophet's life is replete with instances in which he gave of himself to others and was generous in the fullest sense of the term and also of moments of forgiveness of which the conquest of Makkah is the supreme example. This episode demonstrated his nobility of character at its height for he forgave, while he was at the pinnacle of power, those who had wronged him in the worst manner over the years. During certain moments when he acted as judge and did not forgive the wrongdoings of someone, he had the justice of God and the welfare of the community in mind. He acted not as an individual but as a functionary of a human collectivity. Otherwise, there was never a sense of personal vengeance and vindictiveness in his dealings with and treatment of others.

Finally, the Blessed Prophet possessed the virtue of sincerity (*ikhlāṣ*) in its fullness. There is no act which he accomplished or word that he uttered without complete sincerity. But most of all he was sincere with God and his sincerity was the same as truthfulness (*ṣidq*). The fact that he was called al-Amīn, the trusted one, from his youth, means that this quality was present in an eminent fashion in him from childhood and had become perfected when he was chosen as the Prophet of God. Not only the Blessed Prophet never lied, but as a result of this virtue of sincerity and truthfulness, he was able to put each thing in its place, to be logical and objective in his judgment of events, ideas and persons, and to avoid subjective and individualistic distortions. But above all it meant that he was disposed to see the truth and to receive it without changing its nature and content. That is why he was blessed with the knowledge of the most profound of truths, namely *Lā ilāha illa'Llāh*, and chosen to disseminate this central and essential truth on the surface of the earth.

The character of the Blessed Prophet, adorned by the virtues of sincerity, generosity and humility or truthfulness, nobility and simplicity, was also touched by the perfume of kindness and the effusion of happiness by which he is remembered to this day throughout the Islamic world. When the term "Muḥammadan character" (*al-khulq al-muḥammadī* in Arabic or *khūy-i muḥammadī* in Persian and Urdu) is used in various Islamic language, it always implies this sense of kindness and joy combined with the simplicity, nobility and truthfulness already mentioned. When it is said that so and so has *khū* or *khulq-i muḥammadī*, it means that he is blessed by these virtues, that he does not become unnecessarily angry, is calm and collected, has patience and is kind to others. It means that he is in a state of joy and felicity and not given to constant agitation and protest. Muslims do not fail to remember that the Blessed Prophet always smiled and had a sense of happiness and joy emanate from his face which did not of course exclude "holy anger" when he faced those who opposed the Truth. But what is remarkable is that there existed within his soul both vigor and gentleness, both the severity and purity of the desert and the gentle breeze and perfume of a rose garden. He transformed the world and carried out the most remarkable tasks under unbelievable hardships but always with the kindness and generosity which characterizes the friends of God. In him the highest perfections were assembled. He was in reality that perfect man before whom the angels were ordered to prostrate. That is why God and his angels praise and bless him and those who are faithful are commanded to also praise and bless him and to model their lives after him. In fact, the praise of the Prophet is the only act that men shares with God and the angels.

10 The Prophet and Youth

Being at once a father, leader of a community and prophet and founder of a worldwide religion, the Blessed Prophet could not obviously have been impervious to youth and their welfare. On the contrary, all that concerns the young, their upbringing, education, duties obligations and rights were of central importance to him as they are of course to Islam as a whole which he was ordained to bring into the world. The Noble Quran and the *Ḥadīth* are therefore full of references to different questions concerning youth and the *Sharī'ah* contains numerous injunctions which delineate the duties of parents and the community toward the young and also the young towards themselves, their religion, family and the larger social order surrounding them. Moreover, the *Sunnah* of the Blessed Prophet contains numerous elements pertaining specifically to the young and has helped to mold the traditional attitude of Muslim society towards youth in numerous ways.

The most obvious characteristics of the Blessed Prophet's attitude toward the young is his concern and love for them as reflected so clearly not only in the *Ḥadīth* but also in his daily practices as accounted by so many of his companions. The Blessed Prophet loved small children and even when he was already a prophet and ruler of a whole segment of the cosmos not to speak of much of Arabia, he used to play, as already mentioned, with his children, Ḥasan and Ḥusayn—upon them be peace—and even allowed them to ride on his back. He always showed respect for his daughter Fāṭimah—upon her be peace—to the extent of rising before her and greeting her whenever she came before him. According to a well-known saying accounted by none other than 'Ā'ishah, 'I have seen no one more resembling in manner, guidance and conduct of the Noble Prophet than Fāṭimah. Whenever she came to him, he used to stand up for her and then take her by the hand, kiss her and make her sit in his seat. And whenever he went to her, she used to stand up for him, take him by the hand, kiss him and make him sit near her seat." (*Al-Hadis—An English Translation and Commentary of Mishkat-ul-Masabih*, by Al-Haj Maulana Fazlul Karim, Book I. Dacca, East Pakistan, 1960, p. 163—translation slightly modified). He also kissed his children and grandchildren often and enjoined Muslims to do likewise. He ordered them not only to respect their offsprings but to treat them with great kindness including physical caressing and embracing. He emphasized that children were the gift of God to parents and their opt ringing and care was a religious duty and responsibility incumbent upon them. He in fact called children, "the flowers of God."

The Blessed Prophet emphasized especially the care of girls and orphans, two groups of youth most mistreated in the society in which he lived and most likely to be mistreated elsewhere. Because of the very harsh practices against female offsprings in pre-lslamic Arabia, the Blessed Prophet returned again and again in his teachings to the importance of loving one's daughters and treating them well. It seems that God Himself wanted to emphasize for the Islamic community the significance of the female child by giving Fāṭimah—upon whom be peace—as daughter to the Blessed Prophet and by having the whole line of genealogy of the progeny of the Blessed Prophet descend through her. Although without a male heir, he was blessed in the person of Fāṭimah with an offspring of celestial purity who became the mother of not only the eleventh Shi'ite Imams following 'Alī—upon whom be peace—but of the whole community of the *ahl al-bayt* who were to play such a central role in Islamic history.

Having suffered all the hardships of the life of an orphan, the Blessed Prophet was also extremely sensitive to the lot of those children who have to undergo the trying experiences of growing into manhood or womanhood without the protective shield and loving guidance of their parents. It is a result of this emphasis by the Blessed Prophet upon the virtue of treating orphans kindly and of course general Quranic injunctions concerning them that there has been so much attention paid to orphans throughout Islamic history. Perhaps no traditional society has in fact established so many institutions for orphans and emphasized the religiously speaking virtuous character of caring for them as Islam. Behind this general Muslim concern for orphans and the religious injunctions to treat them with compassion is to be seen the special love and affection of the founder of the religion for them

The concern of the Blessed Prophet for youth and their welfare can be best understood by turning to the hierarchy of values in the light of which he promulgated his teachings about the young. The Blessed Prophet emphasized the importance of respect for parents and elders, education and especially *adab*, but he placed at the highest level the love for the Truth, for God, for religion. In the same way that the Noble Quran calls children and property man's enemies if they become our obstacle to the pursuit of His religion and excuses for turning away from the Quranic ethical codes, children are instructed to choose God and His religion even before their parents and family, if it becomes a question of choice. Although it may seem that such a situation would have arisen only in the early Islamic community where many young people had to choose between the polytheistic practices of their parents and Islam, the problem has never disappeared completely. Usually the young learn their religion from their parents and emulate them as their models. The normal transmission of the tradition is from parent to child and in modern times the gradual separation from the sacred mold of Islam appears more among the younger generation in comparison with the older. But there are always cases where the love for God and the desire to practice religion seriously by a particular child or young person is greater than that of one or both parents. The injunction of the Blessed Prophet to choose God even above the dicta or wishes of one's parents becomes particularly significant in such instances and stands therefore as a permanent directive to Muslim youth wherever and whenever they might live.

Respect for parents remains, however, of paramount importance in the Blessed Prophet's teachings about youth and his message to youth. He has in fact said, "No obedient son looks to his parents with a look of kindness but God does not write for him one accepted pilgrimage for every look. They enquired, 'And if he looks a hundred times every day?' 'Yes,' said he, 'for God is greatest and most beneficent.'" (*Mishkāt ul-Maṣābīḥ*, p. 158, slightly revised.)

Parental respect, along with respect for elders in general, issues from obedience to God and love for his Prophet. That is why when parents cease to represent the values of religion in the eyes of their children and no longer practice the teachings of Islam, parental authority dwindles and often results in rebellion of the young against the whole traditional order. Even in cases where parents fail to uphold Islamic norms and principles, however, the Blessed Prophet has recommended the young to respect their parents while not accepting the lukewarm religious views of the older generation. He even ordered those of his disciples whose mothers had not embraced Islam to be nevertheless kind to them. There is in the prophetic message a hierarchy based on a delicate balance according to which the love for Islam comes before even love and respect for parents and yet respect for parents is a duty even if they do not fulfill their religious obligations as Muslim men and women. In such cases the children should pray far their parents as it is their duty to pray for them after their death. When someone asked the Blessed Prophet what he should do for his parents after their death, he replied, "Pray for them and ask for forgiveness for them. Fulfill their promises and wishes after they die."

This delicate question aside, respect and love for parents remains central to the teachings of Islam. The Blessed Prophet left many sayings in which obedience of parents is considered as a key to entry into paradise and the famous *ḥadīth*, "Heaven lies under the feet of mothers (*ummahāt*)," besides its often neglected metaphysical meaning, signifies the great respect the Prophet of God held for mothers. The Blessed Prophet has also said that parents are the heaven and hell of their children, meaning that the attitude of children toward them and their satisfaction with their children or the lack thereof are instrumental in determining the children's mode of posthumous life. Certain spiritual teachers in Islam have in fact made obedience to parents a condition for higher spiritual development. Although this is far from being universal, it nevertheless indicates the spiritual significance that respect and love for parents can have for the final end and spiritual goal of the young Muslim.

Another central element in the teachings of the Blessed Prophet concerning youth is education. If such *ḥadīths* as, "Seeking knowledge is incumbent upon all Muslim males and females," indicates the universality of the obligation to acquire knowledge, "Seek knowledge from the cradle to the grave," emphasizes the early age at which such a process must begin. The virtue of learning and seeking knowledge which became the cornerstone of the traditional Islamic educational system is based on the teachings of the Blessed Prophet and his concern for Muslim youth and the importance of the process of learning in those early years of life when the mental, psychological and physical faculties are most prepared for the transforming experience of education. To love the Prophet means also to love that traditional learning and knowledge which having been ultimately derived from the Noble Quran leads the seeker back to God and is a religious activity.

Complementing the emphasis upon the gaining of knowledge for the young, is the acquiring of *adab*, that combination of courtesy, politeness, good manners, virtue and culture which cannot be translated into a single English word. As the Blessed Prophet has said, "No father can give a better gift to his children than adab," also, "The teaching of *adab* by a man to his children is better for him than great acts of charity.^ In a sense *adab* at its heart coincides with certain aspects of the *Sunnah* and is not just a passing and transient pattern of behavior determined by local cultural conditions. Such relative and local elements exist within the wide domain of *adab* but at its heart lies something of permanent importance for the training of the body and soul of the young Muslim. Its significance is second only to the Truth with respect to which it must, however, remain subservient. Within the realm of adab is included all those virtues with which Muslim youth must adorn themselves. It embraces actions and attitudes which are meant to inculcate within the being of the young humility, generosity, nobility and other virtues found in their fullness in the Blessed Prophet. To sit politely at the table, to greet all people with respect, to discipline one's body while sitting or walking, to speak not only truthfully, but also respectfully, to eat quietly and with dignity and so many other actions and manners included in the traditional Islamic *adab* produce a profound receptivity in the youth for the acceptance of the truths of the tradition, of *al-dīn*. *Adab* in its essence is the manner whereby the Muslim participates in the teachings of the religion within himself or herself, in his or her daily actions and words. That is why along with the gaining of knowledge, the acquiring of *adab* was emphasized so much by the Blessed Prophet and why Muslim parents have been so strongly recommended to teach *adab* to their children.

The concern of the Blessed Prophet for youth involves not only the youth but also their elders. There are a whole series of duties incumbent upon parents and the community at large toward the young. They include first of all loving and caring for them. To earn livelihood for one's children is a religious duty for the father and also the mother, as caring for parents and other older members of the larger family is the duty of the young when they grow old enough to be able to work. Teaching the principles of Islam, the text of the Noble Quran, the daily prayers and later other riles and duties of the *Sharī'ah* is also the religious duty of parents as is the provision of education to the extent possible. The Islamic community as a whole also has this responsibility toward the young. It must provide for their bodily and mental needs as well as the religious guidance which is the matrix within which all the other activities gain their significance.

It is true that the Blessed Prophet and following his example traditional Islamic society have avoided the "youth worship" so characteristic of certain segments of the modern world and have opposed that unbridled so-called "freedom" which has led so many of the young today to a sense of nihilism and meaninglessness of life. It is also true that Islam has emphasized the obligation of the youth before delineating their rights. But this manner of envisaging the needs and conditions of the young do not mean that Islam and the Blessed Prophet who was its perfect embodiment were not interested in them. Rather, it shows how profoundly he was concerned with the young and their deepest needs as Muslims upon whose shoulders the ordering and running of future Islamic society depends at every phase of its history. His instructions are based on the deepest love for youth and their needs which are not only physical but also psychological, intellectual and spiritual. They are promulgated with the goal of enabling the young to gain the only freedom which is meaningful and lasting, the freedom that issues from performing one's duties and obligations toward God, oneself, the family and society in general. Whenever traditional Islamic society has functioned fully, the face of the young has certainly not been without the smile with which God created man, nor has youth become a major problem for society in the way that one observes in the modern world.

11 His *Sunnah* and *Ḥadīth*

Before his death, the Blessed Prophet was asked by what he should be remembered after his departure and he answered by the Noble Quran whose recitation would perpetuate his presence among his community. He also said that he would leave behind him the Noble Quran and his family (*ahl al-bayt*). Actually the Blessed Prophet left behind not only the Book of God and his family, which must be understood both biologically and spiritually, but also his *Sunnah* and *Ḥadīth* which are intimately related to both. The Blessed Prophet left behind a vast treasury of examples of behaving and acting in various circumstances which are called his *Sunnah* and sayings which comprise the *Ḥadīth*, traditions that in Shi'ite Islam include also the sayings of the Imams who are of course the leaders of the *ahl al-bayt*.

The *Sunnah* and *Ḥadīth* of the Blessed Prophet are complements to the Noble Quran and a commentary upon the Book of God. Without them, it would not be possible to understand much of the Book nor even practice the fundamental rites of Islam mentioned in the Noble Quran but only to know their principle and general outline. For example, in the case of the daily prayers, the Sacred Text commands Muslims to perform them (*ṣalli*), but the details of the daily prayers (*ṣalāt* or *namāz*) are based on the Sunnah of the Blessed Prophet. The same is true of fasting, pilgrimage and the like. That is why the *Sunnah* and *Ḥadīth* are, along with the Book of God, the basic pillars of Islam and its Divine Law and have been always considered to be extremely precious and guarded with great zeal. That is also why the attack of modern scholars, including some Muslims mesmerized by the pseudo-scientific claims of historicism, against *Ḥadīth* is so insidious, striking as it does at the very foundation of the Islamic tradition.

The *Sunnah* of the Blessed Prophet as traditionally understood and emulated by generations of Muslims for fourteen centuries is the precious legacy of the founder of Islam and remains inviolable despite all the supposedly scientific and scholarly, but in reality petty and trivial criticisms against it by modernists and agnostics today. This *Sunnah* has many dimensions and facets reaching all the way from the manner of cutting one's nails to facing God in prayer. Some of it is Arab custom, Islamicized through the fact of its adoption by the Blessed Prophet since whatever a prophet, especially a major one, does and says has a significance beyond the historical moment and cultural context in which it originally took place. Other elements of the *Sunnah* are more directly connected with the person of the Blessed Prophet and yet others with the specific form and genius of the Islamic tradition. There is, one might say, a quintessential *Sunnah* which must always be observed in all climes and times in order for the integrity of the Islamic tradition to be preserved and there is a less essential hut recommended *Sunnah* which is of course always revered but which does not possess the same absolutely essential nature. The possibility of the spread of Islam throughout history to different parts of the world and among different peoples is itself proof of this distinction. The essential *Sunnah* has traveled wherever Islam has spread but not certain recommended but non-essential ones which in fact would be sometimes difficult or impossible to follow in certain circumstances. This is of course particularly true in the case of the modern world and of Muslims who have to live in a society which is neither totally Muslim nor even predominantly religious according to another of God's religions.

As for the *Ḥadīth*, it too comprises an ocean of wisdom for all aspects of life. Memorized by the companions and transmitted to later generations, it was scrutinized and examined very carefully by generations of extremely devout scholars, both Sunni and Shi'ites who used every means possible to prevent unauthentic sayings from entering into the corpus of prophetic traditions and who of course were the last people in the world to have forged *Ḥadīth* as some modern critics claim. The result of their unbelievable industry and scholarship is the collections of *Ḥadīth* which have been accepted over the centuries by the Islamic community, six prevalent among the Sunnis and called "The Six Correct Books" (*al-Ṣiḥāḥ al-sittah*) and four among the Ithnā 'asharī Shi'ah, called "The Four Books" (*al-Kutub al-arba'ab*). Although the actual sayings are very similar, the chains of transmission in the two cases are different, a fact which itself confirms the soundness of the methods followed by the scholars of *Ḥadīth* and the authenticity of what they did authenticate according to their respective methods. Also the four Shi'ite books contain the sayings of the Twelve Imams along with those of the Blessed Prophet. Moreover, in both cases the *ḥadīths* are divided into strong, relatively strong, weak, doubtful and totally spurious sayings, and elaborate methods of authentication and analysis have been developed which have made the disciplines connected with the study of *Ḥadīth* one of the most difficult branches of the Islamic sciences.

The *Ḥadīth*, like the *Sunnah*, embrace a vast field and include nearly every aspect of human existence. Some are concerned with the nature of God and worship, others with daily life. They include morality, social and economic life, knowledge and education, the nature of the world, eschatology and the afterlife and the spiritual life. The *Ḥadīth* range from such a tradition as, "God is beautiful and loves beauty," concerning the nature of the Godhead to, "Pay the laborer his wages before his perspiration dries up," involving labor relations. *Ḥadīth*s are an inexhaustible treasury for study and the conducting of human life. They are at once a commentary upon the Noble Quran and a mirror of the mind and soul of the man who was chosen to bring the Word of God to mankind. In fact it is the *Ḥadīth* and *Sunnah*, both written and oral, inscribed in books as well as upon the hearts and souls of men and women, that have enabled Muslims to emulate the Blessed Prophet over the centuries and keep the torch of Islam alive. But the *Sunnah* and *Ḥadīth* are not simply a heritage from an historical past. They are associated with the person of one who is "alive" here and now and who is revered and loved by all Muslims now as he was fourteen centuries ago. That is why while his life has been and is studied and emulated by Muslims everywhere, he himself is praised and benedictions asked upon him and his family in prayers and supplications which themselves have survived the ages and are the fruits of the vision of those illuminated souls who, having emulated the Blessed Prophet, have been blessed by intimacy with his transhistorical reality. From this intimacy has flowed those benedictions and prayers through which Muslims have expressed and continue to express their love and respect for the founder of Islam who is their guide in this world and their intercessor in the world to come.

O my God (*Allāhumma*), bless him from whom derive the secrets and from whom gush forth the lights, and in whom rise up the realities, and into whom descended the sciences of Adam, so that he hath made powerless all creatures, and so that understandings are diminished in his regard, and no one amongst us, neither predecessor nor successor, can grasp him.

The gardens of the spiritual world (*al-malakūt*) are adorned with the flower of his beauty, and the pools of the world of omnipotence (*al-jabarūt*) overflow with the outpouring of his lights.

There existeth nothing that is not linked to him, even as it is said: Were there no mediator, everything that dependeth on him would disappear! Bless him, O my God, by a blessing such as returner to him through Thee from Thee, according to his due.

O my God, he is Thine integral secret, that demonstrateth Thee, and Thy supreme veil, raised up before Thee.

O my God, join me to his posterity and justify me by Thy reckoning of him. Let me know him with a knowledge that saveth me from the wells of ignorance and quencheth my thirst at the wells of virtue. Carry me on his way, surrounded by Thine aid, towards Thy presence. Strike through me at vanity, so that I may destroy it. Plunge me in the oceans of Oneness (*al-aḥadiyyah*), pull me back from the sloughs of *tawḥīd*, and drown me in the pure source of the ocean of Unity (*al-waḥdah*), so that I neither see nor hear nor am conscious nor feel except through it. And make of the Supreme Veil the life of my spirit, and of his spirit the secret of my reality, and of his reality all my worlds, by the realization of the First Truth.

O First, O Last, O Outward, O Inward, hear my petition, even as Thou heardest the petition of Thy servant Zachariah; succor me through Thee unto Thee, support me through Thee unto Thee, unite me with Thee, and come in between me and other than thee: God, God, God! *Verily He who hath imposed on thee the Quran for a law, will bring thee back to the promised end* (Quran, XXVIII:85).

Our Lord, grant us mercy from Thy presence, and shape for us right conduct in our plight. (Quran, XVIII:10).

Verily God and His angels bless the Prophet; O ye who believe, bless him and wish him peace (Quran, XXXIII:56).

May the graces (ṣalawāt) of God, His peace, His salutations, His mercy and His blessings (*barakāt*) be on our Lord Muḥammad, Thy servant, Thy Prophet and Thy messenger, the unlettered Prophet, and on his family and on his companions, (graces) as numerous as the even and the odd and as the perfect and blessed words of our Lord.

Glorified be thy Lord, the Lord of Glory, beyond what they attribute unto Him, and peace be on the Messengers. Praise be to God, the Lord of the worlds (Quran, XXXVII:180-2), ("The Prayer of Ibn Mashīsh," trans. by T. Burckhardt, *Islamic Quarterly*, 1977, pp. 68-69).

Bibliographical Note

Numerous books have been written in European languages since the first polemical works against Islam in the form of biographies of the Prophet appeared in the 5th/11th century in France and Germany. In fact, with the exception of Christ and Napoleon, perhaps no figure has received as much attention by Western biographers as the Prophet. Needless to say, most of these works have been based on either ignorance or prejudice or both. It was not until the 13th/19th century that a number of Western writers began to appreciate, at least to some extent, the grandeur of the Prophet and somewhat more sympathetic biographies began to be written about him although the slanderous treatments of his life also continued unabated. This trend to give a more positive treatment of the Prophet's life has continued into this century with works of such scholars as E. Dermenghem, G. Gheorghiu and W. Watt which deal with some aspects of his life and achievements in a positive light. Meanwhile, several biographies of the Blessed Prophet have been written in European languages by contemporary Muslims such as M. Hamidullah or translated into these languages as in the case of A. Azzam, Z. Rahnema and M. Haykal.

As far as the English language is concerned, however, the most eloquent and moving biography of the Prophet is *Muhammad* by Martin Lings (Vermont:Inner Traditions, 1991) which is recommended highly to those seeking to understand how the Prophet is seen in traditional Islamic sources. We also recommend the work of Annemarie Schimmel, *And Muhammad is His Messenger* (Chapel Hill, the University of North Carolina Press, 1985) which contains a unique selection of translations of devotional literature concerning the Founder of Islam, including both poetry and prose written over the centuries by devout Muslims and reflecting the love and respect which Muslims have always held and continue to hold toward that being whom God addressed in these words, "If thou wert not, I would not have created the heavens" (*law lāk^a wa mā khalaqt^u 'l-aflāk*).

GENERAL INDEX

Other Works by Seyyed Hossein Nasr in English

A Young Muslim's Guide to the Modern World
Three Muslim Sages
Introduction to Islamic Cosmological Doctrines
Science and Civilization in Islam
Ideals and Realities of Islam
Man and Nature
Sufi Essays
al-Biruni: An Annotated Bibliography
Islam and the Plight of Modern Man
An Annotated Bibliography of Islamic Science (3 vols.)
Islamic Science: An Illustrated Study
Persia: Bridge of Turquoise
The Transcendent Theosophy of Sadr al-Din Shirazi
Islamic Life and Thought
Knowledge and the Sacred
Islamic Art and Spirituality
Traditional Islam in the Modern World
The Need for a Sacred Science
Isma'ili Contributions to Islamic Culture (ed.)
Philosophy, Literature and Fine Arts: Islamic Education Series (ed.)
Shi'ism: Doctrines, Thought, Spirituality (ed.)
Expectation of the Millennium (ed.)
Islamic Spirituality: Volume I, Foundations (ed.)
Islamic Spirituality: Volume II, Manifestations (ed.)
The Essential Writings of Frithjof Schuon (ed.)
In Quest of the Sacred (ed.)

Also Available:
The Complete Bibliography of the Works of Seyyed Hossein Nasr From 1958 Through April 1993 prepared by Mehdi Aminrazavi and Zailan Moris